ENJOY
TIME

CATHERINE BLYTH

ENJOY TIME

STOP RUSHING.
GET MORE DONE.

 WHITE LION
PUBLISHING

Brimming with creative inspiration, how-to projects and useful information to enrich your everyday life, Quarto Knows is a favourite destination for those pursuing their interests and passions. Visit our site and dig deeper with our books into your area of interest: Quarto Creates, Quarto Cooks, Quarto Homes, Quarto Lives, Quarto Drives, Quarto Explores, Quarto Gifts or Quarto Kids.

First published in 2018 by White Lion Publishing
an imprint of The Quarto Group
The Old Brewery, 6 Blundell Street
London N7 9BH
United Kingdom

www.QuartoKnows.com

A catalogue record for this book is available from the British Library.

ISBN 978 1 78131 800 3
Ebook ISBN 978 1 78131 801 0
10 9 8 7 6 5 4 3 2 1
2022 2021 2020 2019 2018

Designed and illustrated by Stuart Tolley of Transmission Design

Printed in China by Toppan Leefung Printing Ltd.

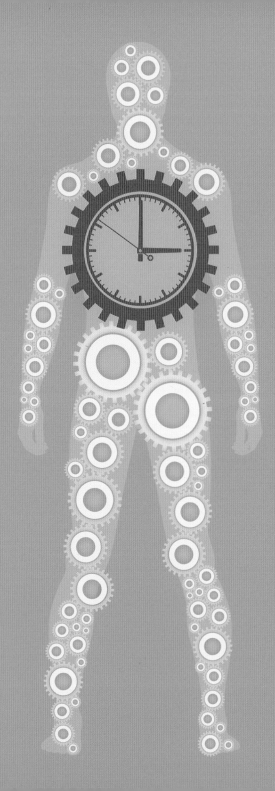

CONTENTS

INTRODUCTION

Enjoy time. Does this suggestion strike you as silly? It's certainly counterintuitive. Generally, we think of time as a commodity (and sadly there's never enough), or a bully (time is pressing), or a faithless lover (there it goes, running out, just when you need it most). We need to make time, spend time, save time, but if by chance we find ourselves with extra time on our hands, then we had better find a way to kill it.

Time is also a vessel that we try to stuff with as many events and efforts as possible, whipped along by our never-ending, ever-expanding, 24/7 to-do list. In fact, many of us are so busy chasing the clock, trying to get up to speed with what we ought to have done, that the notion that time itself might be enjoyable – something sensual, expansive, to curl up in and savour – sounds worryingly like another task to add to that guilt-inducing list.

Yet shouldn't we enjoy time? After all, it's the stuff of life, and in theory we have more time than ever to play around with. Medical and nutritional advances mean that we're living longer than any humans in history, and technology has transfigured the texture and possibilities of what we consider ordinary life. Every moment bursts with potential miracles when space-time barriers fold in the face of a fully charged smartphone. Armed with one of these pocket time machines to teleport your thoughts, desires and cash, you can perform countless complex operations, pretty much instantly, whenever and wherever you please.

Friendships, sex, news, culinary discoveries, musical collaborations, scientific advances, fanbases and business empires mushroom at breakneck speed in the ether of the Net. Better yet, you don't even have to get out of bed, never mind leave home, to join the party.

In these and many more ways your relationship with time has been transformed. Yet this is exactly why it can be difficult to enjoy it.

Another way of looking at the impact of these rapid alterations to everyday experience is that we are under siege. Our attention spans, our desires, our working hours are being bombarded and blasted, splintered and bent into unfeasible shapes by the spiralling, mind-melding distractions, opportunities and obligations that come of living in a blizzard of choice. And the pace of change has left us ill-prepared to grasp and mitigate for the effects on us. Why else does your to-do list keep growing, no matter how hard you prune it? Worse still, multiplying choices can multiply regrets, since for every thing that you decide not to do there is potentially a gnawing legacy – the fear you might have missed out.

Maybe you feel liberated from the restrictions of the past. But freedom weighs heavy if you are glutted. Now that the boundary between work and home, public and private, is perforated by communication technology, guarding the time to call your own is itself a time-consuming challenge.

Another obstacle to enjoying time is

Each of us is a time machine. We can remember our past, be conscious of this moment — right now! — and cast our minds ahead to the future. This lets us see life as a journey.

that the more you consider it, the trickier this elusive thing is to grasp. You can't taste time, or smell it, or hold it. Is it a management tool, a cosmological fact, a stick to beat yourself with, or an intellectual technology that imposes order on the chaos of existence, making life seem like something greater than one damned thing after another?

To me, time is not the enemy. It is all of the above and more – nothing less than humanity's greatest invention. But on a practical, day-to-day level, it is two things: the measurable dimension of being alive, and an organizational device, a bit like a compass. The compass helps you to navigate the dimension: to orientate yourself, to coordinate with others, and to plot your future.

Each of us is a time machine. Unique among the animals, we can remember our past, be conscious of this moment – right now! – as our present, and we can cast our minds ahead to the near and distant future. This lets us see life as a journey, with a direction and destination, empowering us to be so much more than the sum of our daily grind. When we think about who we are, we are all the times of our lives. This is time's finest gift to us. It is also why enjoying time is not a simple question of being more productive, or of seeking ways to escape its pressures.

So don't be time's servant. Let it be your friend on this one-way journey through life.

HOW TO USE THIS BOOK

This book is organized into five parts and 20 lessons covering the key challenges of time and how to manage it.

Each lesson introduces you to an important concept,

and explains how you can apply what you've learned to everyday life.

As you go through the book, TOOLKITS help you keep track of what you've learned so far.

At BUILD+BECOME we believe in building knowledge that helps you navigate your world. So, dip in, take it step-by-step, or digest it all in one go – however you choose to read this book, enjoy and get thinking.

Specially curated FURTHER LEARNING notes give you a nudge in the right direction for those things that most captured your imagination.

TIME IS NO

TIME IS YO

T MONEY.

UR LIFE.

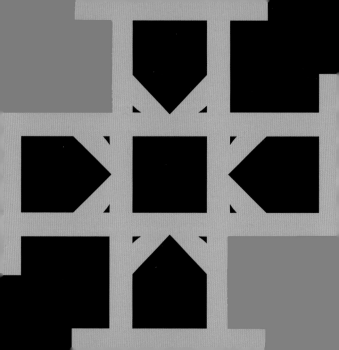

LIVING IN A RUSHOGENIC WORLD

LESSONS

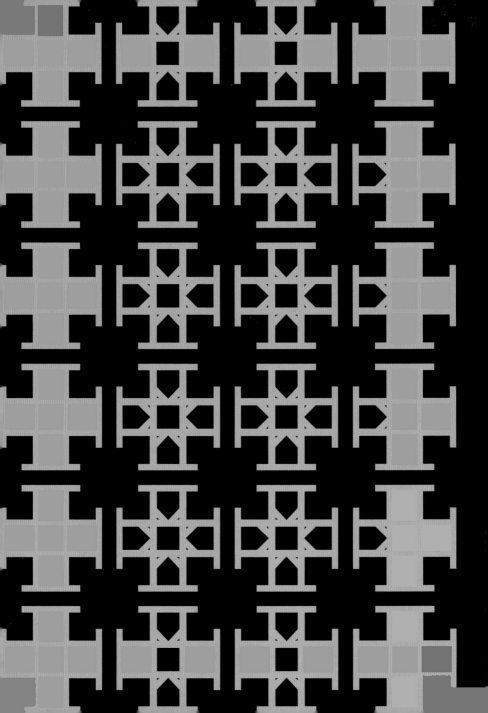

Thanks to technology our relationship with time has altered profoundly. As the linear and sequential are displaced by the instant and simultaneous, this is transforming not only what we can do but who we are.

History tells the story of time's extraordinary power to change lives. Over the past two millennia, innovations in timekeeping acted as an evolutionary accelerant, driving social change. The more precise and ingenious our clocks became, the more precise and ingenious humankind could be. Think of John Harrison's invention of a maritime chronometer with steady enough sea legs to enable ships' navigators to identify longitude as they traversed oceans – opening up trading routes, reshaping civilization.

Time is not just a tool we can use. Timekeeping technology also enables others to control us – from the Chinese emperors whose clocks and calendars allowed them to marshal armies across vast landmasses, to Victorian factories' clocking-in machines, which ensured labourers did not slack off on the shop floor, spurring on the Industrial Revolution. In the twentieth century, wristwatches chopped hours into minutes and seconds, making everyone's time more micro-manageable.

Although we have the greatest potential yet seen on earth to maximize the joys and fruits of our precious hours, it doesn't always feel that way. In today's smart factories – where robots have not yet displaced humans – workers wear technology that monitors their every move, even timing bathroom breaks. And the invention of your bleeping, cheeping smartphone has changed everything. Yes, it places a universe of opportunities in the palm of your hand, but as a result, interruption is the norm, your attention is easily pickpocketed, and your time is less your own.

This chapter explores why we live in a rushogenic world. In the same way that our fast-food culture is obesogenic, making us overweight, so our speed-obsessed culture and technology theoretically free more time, but also encourage us to overstuff it and to rush. Unfortunately, not one of our miraculous gadgets has extended the day by a single second. Instead, we need to take better care of the quality of our time.

FASTER, RICHER AND TIME POORER

We often talk about the pace of life – but what does that mean?

In the 1990s, Robert Levine, a clock-fixated sociologist, returned to the United States from a sabbatical in Brazil, vowing to treat time differently. Rather than lapse into the overscheduling that previously cramped his days as an ambitious academic, he would emulate his new South American friends. Not by adopting their elastic approach to punctuality (he might get fired), but before committing to something, he'd ask himself if he truly wished to do it.

The new habit stuck. And surprisingly often, the answer was yes. Yet although his diary remained full, as if by magic, he felt freer. Being mindful about his time choices let him set the pace.

Fascinated, in 1999 Levine conducted a study of the pace of life in cities and towns in 31 countries around the world. He discovered that walking speed is a pretty reliable indicator not just of a locale's pace, but also its economy, population size and climate. The richer, colder and bigger the place, the faster people strolled, with citizens of London, a wealthy megacity, the world's raciest pavement pounders. Further analysis showed that rapid economic change, cars, communication technologies and an individualistic culture all make for faster societies.

Time seems quicker in a densely populated place because when there's lots going on, this sensory blizzard makes each minute seem fuller and faster, as if time itself were swishing past, stomping and tooting its horn in an agitation of cars and feet. What is

a person to do, confronting such a monster, but hurry up?

If you don't believe the pace of life is speeding up, flash forward to 2009, when a similar study to Levine's discovered the average global walking pace had risen 10% in a decade. Far Eastern cities accelerated most, with Singapore (up 30%) topping the list. It wasn't the richest city, but hurtled up the fast lane, overtaking moneyed London, because its economy had expanded at a higher rate – increasing pressure on workers to keep productive. This is why seemingly lucky beneficiaries of fast-growing economies tend to be less fortunate in another sense, enjoying the least leisure (according to 2011's *European Social Survey* of 23 countries).

You might think that working harder, speeding up, would liberate extra time to do with as you wish. But the reverse is true: the richer you feel, the harder you'll find it to lavish yourself with restorative downtime. Why?

Because an hour feels less disposable to you, the more you earn for it.

External factors contribute to this. Employers' demands intensify as wages go up. What is more, in a thriving economy rising salaries and plentiful overtime make it difficult to justify spending hours you could be paid for on what might feel like frivolous, unpaid activities. In fact, research finds that if you remind someone what he earns per hour this depletes his ability to relax listening to music. This helps to explain why stress levels and cardiac disease are highest in affluent countries.

So how can you escape the hurry trap?

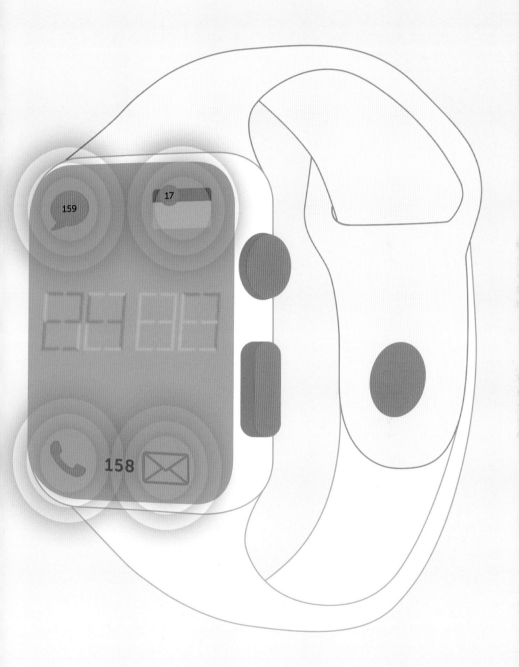

REVALUE YOUR TIME

It's difficult to resist the tug of the world around us and climb off the hamster wheel. It's all too easy to underestimate the value of unpaid hours, to prioritize the paid. But try to remember what you really sell when you sell time. Time is not money. Time is your life: your only medium to be alive in. And it's non-transferable, so why give it away? You'll be time-rich – and most effective – when you redefine urgent and necessary, and stop chasing the clock.

Strangely, subjective wellbeing – that is, the feeling that you are happy – is greatest in fast-paced countries. In other words, people feel happier pursuing a lifestyle that harms them, and it's harm of the type doctors say is most pernicious to health: unpredictable, uncontrollable stress – the stress of a life in which your hours don't feel as if they're yours to command.

Why might stressful hours feel more enjoyable? Well, speed cures boredom, whether in a work-hard-play-hard career, or hurtling up and down a rollercoaster. It's fun – until the point at which you're sick. To thrive, and get more out of your time, you need to compensate for the fact that every human being is exceptionally poor at judging which pleasures are good right now but bad in the long run – and get better at prioritizing.

Are your days filled with junk hours that flash by, leaving little worth remembering – like the nutrition-free junk food that slithers so effortlessly down your throat? Now is the moment to start thinking about time management in the same way you think about nutrition and health. Wellbeing depends on a varied diet: you need downtime, family time, fast times to crack through dull stuff, and slow times to

relax or to concentrate.

Yes, if your day is unrelenting, then flopping in front of the TV at night will seem relaxing. But try to see relaxation as an activity. It's most effective when you're creatively engaged – making something (if only a snack), taking exercise or something manual like knitting. Then be sure to schedule times for these activities.

- If you undervalue your time, price it in a currency that means something to you. Each choice is a trade-off. So if you tend to say yes to everything, adopt a new habit: pause and think what you're saying no to? A good night's sleep? Casual time to catch up with your beloved? These are your opportunity costs. So what matters most?

- Place a higher value on unpaid activities. How do they enhance your motivation? Could you do more of them?

- Slow down. When time starts racing, that's your cue to change pace. Detach from what you're doing, go for a stroll, get a glass of water, find a view to gaze at, do a few stretches. Refreshed, when you snap back into gear, you'll get more of what you want to do done.

I HAVE NO TIME

'Busy.'

I don't know when this became my default reply to the question 'How are you?' But I'm confident it's a poor excuse for a life.

Busy is a word that acts like a shield. It tells other people to expect less of us, and it obscures our choice and responsibility for how we use our day. This can seem convenient, as a license not to do things, and to dodge awkward questions, such as reflecting on how we are, really.

Listen to friends and colleagues and you'll find the busy affliction is catching. We use the word busy as a synonym for productive. We boast about having no time as a badge of honour. Society reinforces these ideals, celebrating concepts like 'me time' because they're luminous exceptions – hours we must battle valiantly to annex from the general rat-run of our lives. This boosts our self-importance, even as it normalizes the idea that aside from this paltry 'me time', our life doesn't belong to us.

Is time poverty actually a hallmark of success? Well, rich people tend to brag about it, but for most of us, economic and social demands mean we feel we have little choice. In fact, the closer you look, the closer time poverty resembles every other type of poverty: it's a form of powerlessness.

How much of your noisy busyness stems from genuine productivity, and how much of it is a delusion, or a mask for your inefficiency?

Oddly, although everyone agrees that time is precious, analyze how we spend it and it's astounding how lightly we give it away. According to 2013's American Time Use survey, the average adult worker's day includes four and a half hours of leisure. They must be lying, right? Nobody has that much time to themselves.

Other statistics reveal why you might not notice those hours leaking away. In 2014 an average British adult invested four irretrievable hours per day watching television, according to Ofcom. That same year, US citizens spent six daily hours on television, an hour on a computer, another hour on a smartphone, plus three more listening to the radio. Often they undertook several of these activities at once, so it amounted to a total of 8 hours 41 minutes on devices – 20 minutes longer than they spent asleep. In other words, more than half their waking hours expired in second-hand, mediated experiences – which are (not coincidentally) less memorable, and less real-feeling, than physical experiences that engage all five senses. Surface from an hour on the Internet, for instance, and you'll feel barely any time has elapsed, busy though your stimulated mind may be.

Of course, 2014 is a Jurassic epoch ago in the digital revolution. Now smartphones thread our days like a sixth sense, so the above figures likely underestimate today's distracted reality.

It's not difficult to see that the texture of life is changing. What's less obvious is that as your sense of time changes, your behaviour changes too.

An intriguing study of 1,500 Dutch people found that those who constantly rush believe time is moving faster. But when time feels fast our reflex response is to rush some more – then we feel busier, time seems faster still, and as we try to out-race it, the odds are that we'll make mistakes. This is how busyness can become a self-perpetuating sensation that sows chaos.

MAKE BUSYNESS PURPOSEFUL

So how can you change for the better? Rushing seldom enhances the quality of output or brings joy. But the philosopher Lars Svendsen, a busyness sceptic, suspects we get attached to the drama of busy to divert ourselves from more disquieting emotions. 'The most hyperactive of us are precisely those who have the lowest boredom thresholds,' he writes in *A Philosophy of Boredom*. 'We have an almost complete lack of downtime, scurrying from one activity to the next because we cannot face tackling time that is "empty". Paradoxically enough, this bulging time is often frighteningly empty when viewed in retrospect.'

Bulging. Frightening. Empty. These are scary words. But fears recede when you build a sense of ownership of time.

- Allocating the right quantity of hours to a task is useless unless you protect their quality. So banish distractions: clear the desk, silence the phone, shut the door.
- When something new bids for your attention, be wary: who says you need to deal with it right now?
- Feel busy and it's easy to imagine you're accomplishing something. So interrogate your busyness. How much of it is because you actually have meaningful things to do? How much of it stems from the sensation of being overloaded? Be alert to that fizzing feeling and next time it strikes, identify the cause. Write down what is stressing you out and you will feel calmer, and may even find you're not as busy as you feel.
- Do you say you're busy to avoid saying no to people? Practise the art of polite but firm refusal – the power of a positive no is wonderfully liberating.
- If you routinely cram your days, are you scared of being bored? Is busyness a decoy, covering feelings of inadequacy? List all the things that you're busy doing then single out activities that give you the greatest sense of accomplishment. Isn't it time you did more of those, and less of the rest?

The worst of busyness is that hunted feeling of hurrying from task to task, like a squirrel in a forest fire, leaping from tree to flaming tree. As you fret about what you must do next, you lose your grip on the now, lessening your pleasure and performance. Don't just prune your schedule: be generous planning the day's transitions. These pockets of time give your mind air to breathe.

PLAN THE D
TRANSITION
THESE POC
TIME LET Y
BREATHE.

AY'S
POINTS.
KETS OF
OUR MIND

HOW TIME PRESSURE SHRINKS THE MIND

'70% off – today only – last three in stock!'

You probably had no idea that you were desperate to buy a handheld, gold-plated, three-cylinder leaf blower – plus tortoiseshell trim and personalized engraving. Not until that helpful email gate-crashed your inbox.

But then you imagine that leaf blower resolutely sending those rotten leaves on their way. . . How could you say no? Nibbling your nails to the quick, you hit the PayPal icon...

'Buy now while stocks last!' is a mighty sales gambit because it employs the most ancient tool of persuasion and desire: scarcity.

'Simply put, people want more of those things they can have less of,' explains Professor Robert Cialdini, author of *Influence*. For this reason, compliance practitioners across the worlds of politics and retail routinely set about enhancing the market appeal of whatever goods they're peddling by making the supply, and the window of opportunity for seizing a piece of it, appear both slender and finite.

How does time pressure charge a dull object with glamour? Convincing you that time is short sets off an emotional tripwire, injecting spurious urgency into a mundane consumer choice. Suddenly it has the character of a drama, with you as the leading actor. The manipulative marketer hopes that part of you will feel not unlike Indiana Jones, watching that gate descend at the entrance to the tunnel, threatening to separate you

forever from your lucky hat (or leaf blower). How could you not reach out and grab it?

When time itself is limited, the logical response is to use it more prudently. As it turns out, time pressure seldom makes better judges of us. On the contrary, as illustrated, it usually causes us to act less rationally.

The reason why we buy and do silly things when we feel rushed is that a scarcity mentality overtakes us, drenching us in stress. In their provocative book, *Scarcity*, Harvard economist Sendhil Maullainathan and Princeton psychologist Eldar Shafir explored poverty and procrastination to show how scarcity is the cognitive equivalent of a poverty trap. Any form of scarcity has the same effect: no matter what resource you lack – biscuits, cash, sun loungers around a hotel pool – the stress caused will 'capture the mind', imposing a cognitive 'bandwidth tax'. For instance, one study asked people with little money to contemplate a hypothetical $1,500 car repair. Their subsequent performance on an IQ test plummeted 13–14 points – equivalent to the mental impairment of one sleepless night. Richer people showed no such damage.

Scarcity leaves you liable to act impulsively, and less mindful of your future interests. Long-term scarcity impairs your thinking in the longer term too. According to neurological scans, sustained stress damages the brain area devoted to goal-focused decisions and actions. Worse still, it enhances the part in

charge of forming habits. This is because when we feel overloaded, we release dopamine, epinephrine, noradrenaline: neurotransmitters that encourage rash, addictive behaviour. 'Thus, the part of the brain that enables creative problem solving becomes less available the more we need it,' wrote behavioural psychologist Walter Mischel, an expert in self-control.

In some cases time pressure can be handy. There's truth to the cliché that if you want a job done, give it to a busy person. When working to a strict deadline, your intellectual horizon narrows, driving you into what psychologists call a cognitive tunnel, but this concentrates your attention and, like Indiana Jones, you won't rest until it's done, zoning in on only what is absolutely necessary.

The drawback is that inside a cognitive tunnel you lose perspective: you'll be 'less insightful, less forward-thinking, less controlled', as Maullainathan and Shafir put it. From a neurological perspective, you're in a fight-or-flight state, in which you will tend to grab the nearest resource that looks like an answer to your problem.

MAKING TIME PRESSURE WORK FOR YOU

Perhaps you've never panic-bought anything costlier than a roll of toilet paper. Even so, you can't afford to ignore the dastardly effects of time pressure. Thanks to proliferating distractions and e-commerce, you're frequently exposed to cues seeking to massage a sense that time is running out – and interruptions make time shorter, just by snapping your attention.

Get in the habit of feeling chronically short of time and the price can be high. A 2008 survey found that only 6% of respondents who identified as busy cut back on work, while 57% cut back on hobbies and 30% on family time – those irreplaceable things that restore us and make time feel full.

If time is scarce, the onus is on you to be discerning about how you use it and override that scarcity mentality.

Time pressure – such as a deadline – can be fruitful. If it's well calibrated it creates predictable, controllable stress, the kind that's good for your heart. So take control of the pressure, structuring your day with regular, small goals. Vary the pace, especially in the afternoon, as your perception of time speeds up and concentration fades. Attend to when time pressure works, when it gets too much, and you might start enjoying it. If nothing else, build your tolerance of time pressure and it will be less stressful – making it harder for others to drive you into cognitive tunnels.

- Plan your schedule when you're relaxed and you'll make better choices, in your own good time.
- Track how much time you invest in hobbies, family, friends, versus work. When during the week do you routinely face difficult choices? Assess them (in a non-pressured moment, perhaps over the weekend). If the cumulative pattern worries you, experiment. What happens if you leave the office on time for a week, or spend longer over a family breakfast? Are you more or less effective?

- Be alert to artificial time pressures: why is there a deadline? Serving whose convenience? Is it authentic? If that retailer's discount code expires at midnight, what are the chances they won't email a new one next week?
- Create an environment in which it's easier to recognize you've entered a cognitive tunnel. Record how much time bleeds on diversions or dealing with emergencies. How many distractions are exacerbated by unnecessary rushing – leading you to give them undue weight, at an inconvenient moment?

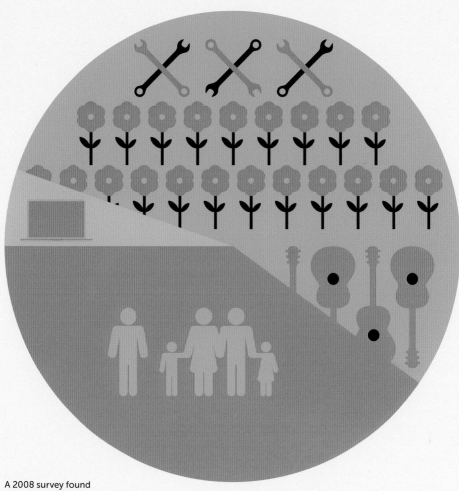

A 2008 survey found that only 6% of respondents who identified as busy cut back on work, while 57% cut back on hobbies and 30% on family time.

24/7 SOCIAL JETLAG

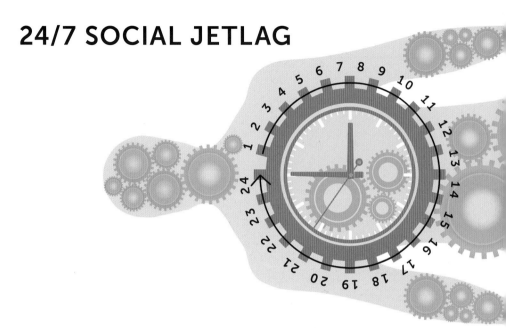

Economists rejoice at the wealth created by 24/7 living. But does it enrich you?

As newborn babies demonstrate, it takes a while to master a steady daily rhythm, in tune with the world around you. Disrupt it and you won't feel great; and reclaiming it is tough, as soaring numbers of insomniacs will tell you. And this task is getting harder because the architecture of time in our lives is being dismantled. Lunch breaks, opening hours and TV schedules once paced our days, giving society a communal rhythm. Then smartphones, box sets and all-night burger joints came along, tempting us to work, rest and play from dusk till dawn.

How to fit it all in? Sadly, despite the 24/7 lifestyle that technology encourages, we still, internally at least, have a Stone Age metabolism, which evolved over hundreds

of thousands of years, programmed by our habitat, so continues to be defined by the stubborn limits of the 24-hour period in which our planet rotates on its axis. But nowadays it's a rare soul who rises and goes to bed with the sun, and this sets our physiology at odds with our culture. The net result is social jetlag, which is bad news for your body clock.

The body clock is complicated. Chronobiologists, who specialize in this branch of science, are just beginning to comprehend how our physiological rhythms interact in an intricate metabolic dance that underpins wellbeing. In 2017, Jeffrey C. Hall, Michael Rosbash and Michael W. Young received a Nobel Prize for identifying the molecular mechanisms that regulate 24-hour circadian rhythms (from Latin's *'circa'*

– about; *'diem'* – a day). It's hoped their discoveries will open the door to medical treatments for the worst damage caused by the chronic misalignment between modern lifestyles and our native tempo.

To picture your body clock, imagine a huge number of interlocking cogs. Each cog represents a different cycle, from the 28-day menstrual cycle, to the 90- to 120-minute bursts of sleep that string together a night's rest. These cycles constitute the repair and working schedules of your vital organs. Particularly important are your circadian rhythms. The most conspicuous are your sleep cycle, hunger phases, and the peristaltic timetable that sends you scurrying to the loo after breakfast. Yet subtler cycles matter just as much, for blood pressure, body temperature, and manufacturing hormones and enzymes. Even your immune system functions better at certain hours – hence when you take medication affects its efficacy (before noon is best for the elderly).

Homeostasis is the word for that happy equilibrium when all cycles are balanced. But if one cog turns too fast or slow, your whole system is affected.

Put in long working days, deny yourself sleep, and yes, you may pat yourself on the back for your industry. What you can't see are the accumulating penalties of upsetting your innate tempo. But hair-raising data shows that shift workers and airline crew are 40% likelier to suffer cardiovascular disease. Other risks include cancer, diabetes, obesity, memory loss, gastro-intestinal disorders and prematurely aged brains.

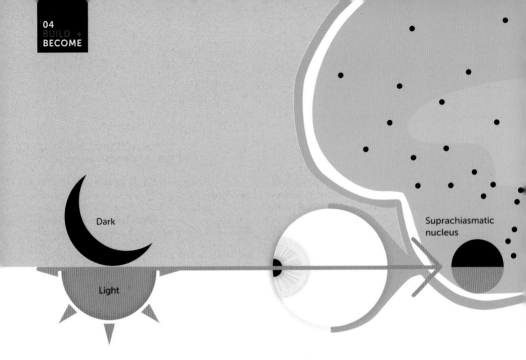

Dark

Light

Suprachiasmatic
nucleus

RESTORE YOUR TEMPO

Forget medical treatments. Living in sympathy with your native rhythms is the fast path to wellbeing. And if your body clock is out of whack, you can restore those cogs to best practice. Primarily by being clever about when you sleep, encounter light and eat.

01. Sleep cycle

As those Nobel winners discovered, numerous peripheral clocks are stationed in your body, controlled by genes, molecules and cells. But one master clock coordinates them all: the suprachiasmatic nucleus (SCN), a nub of 20,000 nerve cells above your optic nerve. Light is its on-off switch. As darkness falls your SCN triggers your brain to produce chemicals, such as serotonin, preparing for sleep. The SCN also synchronizes your other time cycles, which is why, without light, your body clock may unravel.

Most of us see too much light, not too little. Consequently, we miss sunshine's natural sleep cues. Light itself is not bad; the issue is when you're exposed to it. A few hours' intense radiance on a wintry morning, for instance, can lift low moods. But staring at laptops and smartphones after dark confuses the SCN, because they emit high-frequency blue light, similar to daylight. As a result, the brain is not stimulated to produce the serotonin that makes you drowsy – a bad idea, since serotonin is synthesized into melatonin, nature's wonder drug, which slows ageing, reduces stress, cholesterol, melancholy, and suppresses tumour growth. Long-term sleep disruption and light exposure weaken the SCN's ability to coordinate the body clock – with grim consequences, according to neuropsychologist Randy Nelson: 'The increasing rate of depressive disorders in

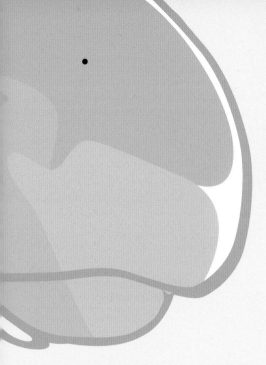

As dark falls, the suprachiasmatic nucleus stimulates the brain to produce chemicals that make you drowsy, preparing for sleep.

IF YOU FEEL LOW, OR
STRUGGLE TO SLEEP
01. Be strict about when you expose yourself to light — more in the mornings, please
02. Hit the dimmer switch at night
03. Banish smartphones and laptops for an hour before sleep (don't charge them in your bedroom)
04. Keep your bedroom cool (sleep is intertwined with your body temperature; as it declines, you become sleepy)
05. Avoid evening exercise (you will be too hot) and late-night stimulants: coffee, computer games, horror movies
06. Cultivate bedtime rituals

TO EAT YOUR BODY CLOCK
BACK IN SYNC
01. Abolish midnight feasts
02. Consume most calories early, aiming to fast for 12 hours through the night
03. In the evening, pick foods rich in tryptophan, a source of serotonin: nuts, tofu, poultry

humans corresponds with the increasing use of light at night in modern society.'

02. Food cycle
You are when you eat. 'The time we eat determines when a particular gene turns on or off,' explained Satchidananda Panda, Professor of Regulatory Biology at the Salk Institute. Your liver's metabolism is ruled by the epigenome — a set of molecules instructing genes when and how many proteins to produce. Gobble that 3 a.m. kebab and this switches on a gene that should only work during the day. What is more, your pancreas releases glucagon at night, stimulating a gene (CRTC2) that instructs your liver to produce glucose, so eating late risks glucose overload. 'It's like over-charging a car battery,' says Panda. 'Bad things happen.' Such as obesity, diabetes, heart disease and kidney failure.

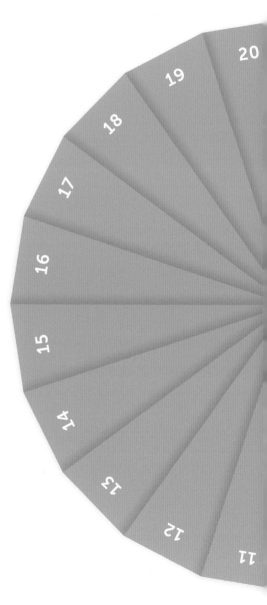

TOOLKIT

01

Society is accelerating. Yet as life's pace speeds up and we grow more prosperous, we undervalue our time, treating it as a commodity. As a result, health, happiness and family life suffer. But slowing down is hard. So think about time as you would about nutrition and health. If you face a difficult decision, question the potential trade-offs: is overtime more important than an evening at home?

02

Time poverty is not a sign of success but powerlessness. Buy into the no-time myth and other people will expect less of you, trapping you in a busy loneliness. Although many people feel overwhelmed, most of us squander time on distractions. So be a busyness sceptic and learn to distinguish genuine busyness from disorganisation and panic.

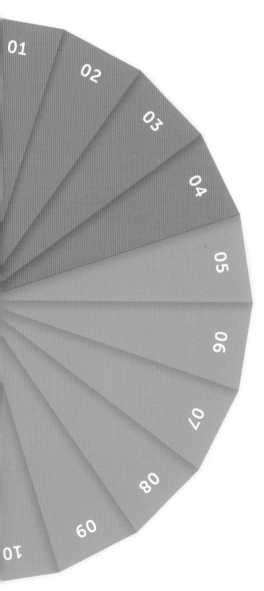

03

Time pressure is a great marketing tool. Businesses use it to trick consumers into a scarcity mindset, triggering a stress state that drives us into a cognitive tunnel, making us impulsive. Raise your awareness of bogus time pressures, noticing when you get trapped in that tunnel and lapse into short-term thinking. Practise using time pressure mindfully to benefit from the upside of stress.

04

Human beings evolved in duet with our environment, so your body clock is attuned to the sun's rise and fall. But light pollution and our 24/7 economy disrupt it, creating social jetlag. This interferes with your sleep, metabolism and brain, at a huge cost to your health. Protect your natural rhythms and sleep cycle by avoiding artificial light and technology in the evening, and eating in daylight hours.

FURTHER LEARNING

READ

Influence
Robert Cialdini (HarperBusiness, 2007)

Faster
James Gleick (Abacus, 2000)

Pip Pip: A Sideways Look at Time
Jay Griffiths (Flamingo, 2000)

A Geography of Time
Robert Levine (Oneworld, 2006)

Why We Sleep
Matthew Walker (Penguin, 2018)

WATCH

Satchidananda
Dr Satchin Panda on time-restricted feeding
www.foundmyfitness.com/episodes/satchin-panda

HumanKinda, a short film about busyness
www.fastcompany.com/3052562/see-how-ridiculously-busy-we-all-are-in-humankinda-a-short-film-from-jetblue

DO

myCircadianClock
This app, designed by Satchin Panda and Emily Manoogian, tracks your daily patterns, offering insights into your body's rhythms and advancing scientific research.

HOW TIME CHANGES SPEED

LESSONS

We are all dancers to the music of time. We have an incredible ability to synchronize with the beat of our environment.

When time speeds up or slows down, something inside you changes.

Consider how your feelings morph while you are watching a movie. Film director Alfred Hitchcock well understood how to control his audience's emotions. Remember how stealthily, how slowly, that dagger moves towards the shower curtain in *Psycho* while Janet Leigh rinses her hair? The stabbing soundtrack shrieks: *Eek! Eek! EEEK!*

This masterclass in suspense illustrates three points. First, fear slows time. Second, scary music makes it seem slower still. Third, slow time is itself scary.

The following lessons examine how and why our time perception fluctuates. When it seems to speed up or slow down, how does that affect you, and why does this matter? Appreciate its influence on how you move, think, feel, eat and spend your money, and

it becomes abundantly clear that we are all dancers to the music of time. We have an incredible ability to synchronize with the beat of our environment, yet can be frighteningly feeble at resisting its impact on our emotions and actions. Hurrying even affects how much we care about other human beings. But understanding these forces, learning how you are manipulated, unlocks exciting possibilities for enhancing your memory, mood and pace.

Digital technology, phones and computers not only colonize time, they also weaken concentration and willpower, but we're stuck on them thanks to our addictive brain chemistry. However, distractibility is a valuable feature that allowed our agile, adaptable species to take over planet earth. Learn to manage distraction, strengthen your attention, and you can cascade positive change in your life.

TIME WARPS

Everybody has experienced instant hours and marathon minutes – from the 1,000-year chat with your boss at the office party, to the evening that vaporized in seconds, playing computer games. These time warps occur because time's speed is a purely subjective perception. As Albert Einstein, who discovered space-time, put it: 'An hour with a pretty girl on a park bench passes like a minute, but a minute sitting on a hot stove seems like an hour. That's relativity.'

Quite literally, your brain makes up time as you go along, estimating its passage by snatching at clues. Just as you see a breeze indirectly in the skittering of leaves on the lawn, so time is detectable through changes in your environment. Anything that produces a contrast that you can perceive is a temporal marker, evidence that your brain interprets as proof that time is moving on.

Since your sense of time is a by-product of your mental processes, when its pace seems to change this means that something has shifted in how you are paying attention. You needn't be consciously aware of it for your brain to register it: even a shift as subtle as music changing pitch will increase cognitive activity. And the more thinking you do within a given moment, the slower that moment – or that piece of music – will seem. But once that melody is familiar, then the next time you hear it, the pitch change will provoke fewer thoughts. As a result the music will seem faster – essentially, because it interests you less. Alas, this doesn't mean that uninteresting things always appear fast. On the contrary, when you're bored, time positively crawls, as you exhaust mental and emotional energy longing for the tedium to be over.

Temporal markers are incredibly important, as reference points to help you orientate as you navigate the world. They matter more in some situations than others. Crossing the road, for example, is lethal unless you assess the speed of oncoming vehicles accurately. But just walking along the street, your brain constantly parses temporal cues, adjusting your pace accordingly, a fantastically fiddly neurological manoeuvre that you hardly notice – not until it goes wrong and you bump into somebody.

Other time warps are activated by our emotions, especially intense sensations such as fear. When we are in danger, time really seems to hit the brakes, as Nelson Mandela discovered. For two years, he was South Africa's most-wanted political fugitive, fleeing from safe house to safe house, living in fear of the brutal Apartheid regime. But for him, one of the longest moments of these dark days transpired in under a minute, while waiting at traffic lights when he saw a colonel from the local Security Branch in the next car. 'He never looked my way,' Mandela remembered, 'but even so, the seconds I spent waiting for the light to change seemed like hours.'

During these protracted seconds Mandela entered hyper-alert, flight mode. His brain flooded with noradrenaline, causing it to fire extra neurons, increasing neuronal activity and accelerating his perceptions – in effect, affording him extra thinking time per second to decide how to respond to the threat.

This time warp shows how emotions alter your sense of time as nothing else can. After all, that is their job: they are chemical signals and their purpose is to influence your behaviour.

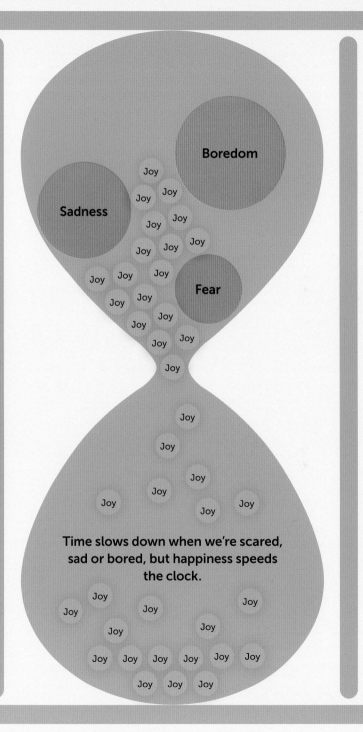

Boredom

Sadness

Joy
Joy
Joy
Joy
Joy
Joy
Joy
Joy
Joy
Joy

Fear

Joy
Joy
Joy
Joy
Joy

Joy

Joy

Joy

Joy
Joy
Joy
Joy
Joy

Time slows down when we're scared, sad or bored, but happiness speeds the clock.

Joy
Joy
Joy
Joy
Joy
Joy
Joy
Joy
Joy
Joy
Joy
Joy
Joy

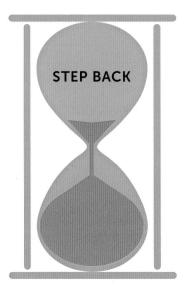

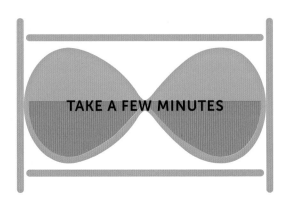

STEP BACK

TAKE A FEW MINUTES

READ THE SIGNS

Notice how time flows and you can learn a lot about what is going on inside you. Your feelings are incredibly powerful, but you can use them as a tool. Attend to your emotional response and this can point the way to making time richer.

For instance, when you are feeling low, your brain is starved of dopamine, the happiness neurotransmitter. As a result, time itself will seem to dawdle, and your brain will absorb fewer details, making life seem hollow indeed – entrenching that low mood.

It can be just as damaging to psychological health if time always seems too speedy. Maybe you live in an accelerated universe, because you frenetically ward off

boredom, operating on multiple channels – talking, scrolling, texting, never listening. Yet if life passes like a blur of images glimpsed from a runaway train, how will you precipitate the memories that make it seem meaningful?

Interestingly, although happy occasions dash by, they seem long in retrospect. This is because different emotions forge different types of memory. When you're happy, your dopamine-bathed brain sends your attention fluttering about like a butterfly, but you also take in lots of peripheral details. Hence a great party always ends too soon, yet leaves a long and satisfying afterlife, trailing crowds of rich, detailed memories. So it really is worth enjoying time. It feels better spent.

SAVOUR THE MOMENT

If life passes like a blur of images glimpsed from a runaway train, how will you precipitate the memories that make it seem meaningful?

Who says happy times have to be over in a flash? Step back during that joyful occasion, take a few minutes to reflect on its significance and consciously observe what is going on. I did this on my wedding day. Not only did time slow down, giving me longer to savour it, but those burnished perceptions still glow in memory's amber, years later.

- When time seems dreadfully slow, or unnervingly fast, what does this reveal? Is an organic factor responsible – when did you last eat, exercise or have a good night's sleep? Does that sluggish time say something about your mental state? Understand the cause and you have a guide for change.
- Perhaps you need to approach the situation differently. Seek opportunities within it. Meeting that new area manager may never be fun, but could be viewed as a chance to hone social skills. Why not treat it as a game: five points for each time you make him smile.
- Or perhaps you could alter the situation: can you introduce a different dimension, vary the ingredients, make it more novel? Would swapping this activity to a different hour make it easier to engage (for example, the morning, when you're most alert)?

WHO CONTROLS YOUR TEMPO?

If you're down, time is not the only thing that seems slower. Don't your feet also weigh heavy, as if your shoes were lined with lead? This is because your perception of time does not just seem faster or slower, according to your changing mood; when time's speed seems to change, that affects how fast you move. What this means is that both your tempo and emotions can be easily manipulated – by yourself and other forces. The good news is that if you change your tempo, you can reset your emotions. Take that early morning run – it raises your heartbeat, releases endorphins, lifts your spirits and makes time march to a sprightlier beat.

Even incredibly subtle influences have an impact on our behaviour. In one experiment, test subjects were flashed images of fast-food logos so fleetingly that they didn't consciously see them. Subsequently they read a text significantly faster than subjects who had not been exposed to these subliminal cues.

Music is far less subtle, but exceptionally potent at shifting our emotional gears. In another fascinating study, happy, upbeat songs were played to happy students, and sad, slow songs to unhappy students, as well as the reverse: upbeat songs to sad students, downbeat songs to the happy. Afterwards almost all participants reported that their mood changed in line with the music's emotional signature, but this shift was strongest if their initial feelings were the *opposite* of the song's. The academic term for this is 'congruence effects'.

Music doesn't just alter inner states. In another experiment at a Scottish half-marathon, when fast music played over loudspeakers the runners sped up, but if its tempo slowed, they did too. Why? Because all human beings are wired to match the

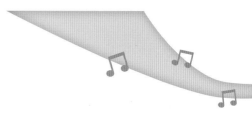

tempo around us. This phenomenon, known as entrainment, leads us to synchronize with any rhythm or beat in our environment. You may not be aware of it, but it governs swathes of your life. It's what's going on when you fall in with the pace around you, and the reason why you would struggle to mooch on Manhattan's sidewalks alongside bustling New Yorkers, but in the Serengeti, you would slow to a Masai saunter.

If entrainment helps you keep up with the crowd, it also makes you vulnerable, since it means that your pace, mood and behaviour can be manipulated, drawn like magnets by environmental factors. It happens all the time, without you even noticing, because entrainment is a boon to business.

Thanks to generations of market researchers, we know that up-tempo beats usher people faster around the shops, raising their spend per minute. A further commercial advantage of music is that even the softest noise absorbs cognitive capacity – literally making it harder to hear yourself think, or to

repress the urge for an impulse buy.

No surprise, then, that low-cost, high-volume food outlets favour uplifting pop. Not only does it fill burger joints but it empties them quicker too, because customers eat faster, in time with the beat.

Interestingly, the economic benefit of fast versus slow music depends on the context. A study in a mid-range Texan restaurant discovered that although pacy music increased the turnover of tables, slower melodies encouraged patrons to linger longer in the queue, and to drink more once they finally sat down. This upped profits overall, since the mark-up on beverages is higher than on food. Similarly, larger supermarkets tend to serenade shoppers with tranquil music to coax them into lingering in those aisles, because if they take more time, ultimately they buy more. So it turns out that a slower pace will not necessarily make you more discerning or self-controlled, proving that there are times when the hare can beat the tortoise.

01

CONTROL YOUR PACE

Entrainment is deep in your bones. It began after you were born and lay in your mother's arms, when your breathing and your heartbeat synchronized in a duet with hers. Keeping pace is also a sensible evolutionary adaptation, ensuring that you coordinate with the world around you without getting left behind. But open your ears and eyes and as you roam through the landscapes of your life, you will soon detect the devious forces bent on controlling your pace, mood and spending.

Become sensitized to how your pace and emotions are manipulated, for better and for worse, and you can adapt your behaviour to counter it. You also gain a set of tools. Why not stage your own tempo hack?

Many creatives, from musicians to mathematicians, ascribe their success to coffee. If you see the tangled cobweb that a caffeinated spider will produce, you might question whether caffeine orders the mind, but it definitely makes time seem speedier.

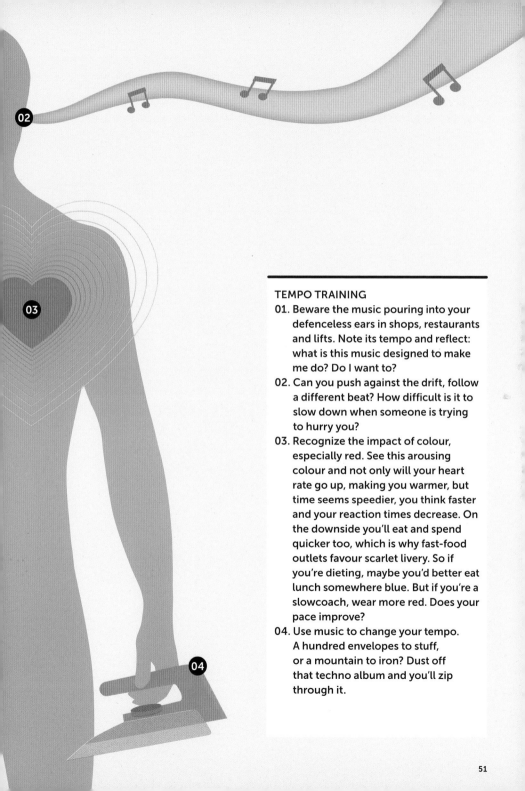

TEMPO TRAINING

01. Beware the music pouring into your defenceless ears in shops, restaurants and lifts. Note its tempo and reflect: what is this music designed to make me do? Do I want to?

02. Can you push against the drift, follow a different beat? How difficult is it to slow down when someone is trying to hurry you?

03. Recognize the impact of colour, especially red. See this arousing colour and not only will your heart rate go up, making you warmer, but time seems speedier, you think faster and your reaction times decrease. On the downside you'll eat and spend quicker too, which is why fast-food outlets favour scarlet livery. So if you're dieting, maybe you'd better eat lunch somewhere blue. But if you're a slowcoach, wear more red. Does your pace improve?

04. Use music to change your tempo. A hundred envelopes to stuff, or a mountain to iron? Dust off that techno album and you'll zip through it.

YOUR TEMP
WHO YOU A
SO STOP R
NOW SET

O CHANGES
RE.
USHING.
OUR PACE.

MESSAGE ALERT!

Don't you hate it when there's a fly in the room? And isn't it funny how you only ever notice that fly, bouncing off the windows, when you need to focus on something else?

When your brain is captured by an irrelevant thing, you have fallen victim to what is called 'involuntary attention'. But unwelcome as your distractibility may be, it has practical benefits. How else could your agile senses monitor multiple matters simultaneously – zooming in instantly at the sound of your name uttered on the other side of the room, or detecting that whiff of smoke before the house goes up in flames?

'Distraction is the price we pay for being able to focus on an event of interest while also gleaning information from other sources,' explained cognitive psychologist Professor Dylan Jones. 'This arrangement has the undoubted advantage of allowing flexibility and adaptability.'

Distractibility's drawback is that, with the onslaught of modern technology, the faintest quiver of a muted smartphone can hijack your attention. You may resent the interruption, or stifle the urge to check instantly; even so, you'll probably feel excited because that message alert

registered in your brain as a novelty, causing it to fire dopamine, the happiness neurotransmitter.

The problem with dopamine is that your brain habituates to it rapidly, so you'll crave ever higher, ever more frequent doses in order to sustain your jolly mood. Thus with little ado, you slip into the noose of a dopamine loop, grazing message after message, and before you know it you're stuck on what psychologists describe as a 'hedonic treadmill'. This is similar to entering

a fight-or-flight state: you'll snatch for the next novelty as if it were your last. In other words, dopamine, a perfectly legal high, is hideously addictive, fuelling shoppers, gamblers, online gamers, iPad-hypnotized toddlers and social media junkies. Most of the profits made on the Internet rely on it. How much of your life is defined by it? What an irony that communication technology markets itself as a way to save time.

These aren't the only neurological problems caused by our ubiquitous digital distractions. You may not be aware of the fact that when you interface with a screen, text or email you tend to hold your breath or to breathe shallowly, often hunching your body too. This deprives your brain of oxygen, tipping it into a stress response, also akin to fight-or-flight mode. But although you are awash with stress hormones, you are doing nothing physical to burn them off. So what happens next? You get jittery, time seems faster and the compelling rewards of that dopamine loop get even less resistible – making you ever more distractible.

Distraction does not just suck away time by pulling your train of thought off its tracks; you'd be amazed how much mental energy is lost in the effort to lasso it back, gnawing invisibly at your concentration, willpower and productivity. Professor Gloria Mark, an expert on this topic, calculated that on average workers concentrate for three minutes before something snips their mental thread. Another 2011 study estimated that U.S. companies employing over 1,000 workers lose $10 million a year to employees' minds being hoovered up by social media. This figure is climbing steeply, and our attention spans are shrinking commensurately.

BEATING DISTRACTION

You owe your life to distractibility. If your restless ancestors hadn't been alert, nosy, sensation-seekers, with minds magnetized by their dopamine rewards system to find new things fascinating, they wouldn't have been responsive enough to potential threats or opportunities to survive and bequeath you your distractible genes. So how can you use this trait for good in your daily life?

Sometimes distraction is stimulating. Working in a cluttered space has been shown to help compost richer thoughts (good news for messy people). Perhaps you love hot-desking in cafés, on the grounds that it froths up your inspiration. Well, you're not entirely wrong; gentle ambient noise can help trigger original ideas. So the next time you want to brainstorm, pick a lively spot. But don't be tempted to stick around once the moment comes to knuckle down. Neither the companionable muttering of colleagues, nor that discreetly rustling newspaper at the neighbouring table will aid your concentration. Laboratory experiments conducted by Professor Dylan Jones confirm that extremely low levels of background noise zap the brain's performance by 20 to 30%. In a non-laboratory setting like a busy, open-plan office, the draining effects must be significantly greater.

Your adorably addictive attention-hooking media devices are not predisposed to strengthen your concentration. Sadly, the more distracted you are – the more frequently your involuntary attention is tugged hither and thither – the trickier it becomes to command your voluntary attention.

How to avoid overload? Your brain's natural reaction is to dump cognitive cargo. That is why you get forgetful when you're stressed or have too much on, yet can ruthlessly focus on the most relevant matters under a tight deadline. Willpower decays over the course of each day (hence it's easier to tackle tricky tasks in the morning), and also dwindles through use. So the more effort you spend on refocusing after interruptions, the shorter your attention span gets. To lengthen it, and thrive in this world without limits, you need to impose limits of your own.

- Be mindful of your environment. Shut the door, silence the radio.
- Ration distractions. Set times to check emails or Facebook.
- Make the most of your willpower in the morning, the best time for demanding tasks.
- Build concentration. Track how many uninterrupted minutes you focus. Can you go longer tomorrow?
- Punctuate the day with rewards to repair willpower. A snack after one unbroken hour at your desk? A five-minute Snapchat binge after two?
- If your eye keeps coasting to your phone, upload Forest App. The longer you ignore it, the more trees grow – but answer a call before your allotted time is up and watch those good intentions wither.

MONDAY 20TH JUNE

10:00	10:15	10:30 **Break**	10:45
11:00	11:15	11:30	11:45
12:00	12:15 **Break**	12:30	12:45
13:00	13:15	13:30	13:45
14:00	14:15	14:30	14:45 **Break**
15:00	15:15	15:30	15:45
16:00 **Break**	16:15	16:30	16:45
17:00	17:15	17:30	17:45

SLOWING DOWN VERSUS RUNNING LATE

You're late, again. There goes the bus, and there goes your chance of catching the 11.06 and arriving at that interview on time. On balance, you decide to run for it. The question is, as you sprint to the train station, where is your head?

In a hurry your thoughts will scurry. No matter how smart a thinker you might be, speed bludgeons the wits, as renowned psychologist Daniel Kahneman confided in his book *Thinking, Fast and Slow*:

'Accelerating beyond my strolling speed completely changes the experience of walking ... [bringing] about a sharp deterioration in my ability to think coherently. As I speed up, my attention is drawn with increasing frequency to the experience of walking and to the deliberate maintenance of the faster pace.'

Although your mind is always travelling forwards and backwards through time, your physical actions determine its direction of travel – quite literally. One study found that if a person sits on a train, facing ahead, their thoughts naturally incline to future plans. But if their seat faces backwards then, as they watch the world recede, their mind drifts to the past.

Not surprisingly, when hurrying to a destination, your fractured thinking focuses on that urgent future. It is almost as if you imagine that by fixating on where you want to

be – RIGHT NOW! – you can wing your heels and reach it sooner. But time also seems to rush, upping your stress levels accordingly. So anything standing between you and your goal had better watch out...

Sound brutal? Well it is. Hurry always tips you into a future-oriented mood, locked on what lies ahead, diminishing your sense of the world around you. What is less obvious is that as hurry contracts your mental horizon, your ethical bandwidth narrows too. This was proven by the unexpected results of a seminal experiment from the annals of social psychology.

Inspired by the parable of the Good Samaritan, in 1973 psychologists John Darley and Daniel Batson hoped to discover which personality traits, if any, would predict helping behaviour. So they recruited trainee priests from Princeton's seminary to complete a questionnaire, designed to reveal their moral character (had they chosen priesthood out of ambition or a vocation, for instance). Then they were sent to another building to write a speech, either on the neutral subject of jobs at the seminary, or on the Good Samaritan parable. Some trainees were advised they were running late, others that they had a few minutes to spare.

Now came their real, secret test. Between the two buildings was an alley. In it a man lay,

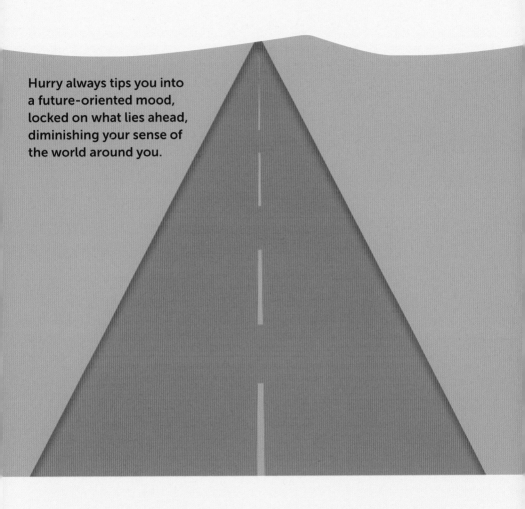

Hurry always tips you into a future-oriented mood, locked on what lies ahead, diminishing your sense of the world around you.

moaning and coughing. Would they help him?

Some trainees stopped, some didn't. No surprise there. But what shocked Darley and Batson was that neither having a spiritual personality, nor having kind thoughts planted in their minds (those tasked with writing about the Samaritan), made a jot of difference. Only one thing mattered: if the trainees believed they were late they hoofed on by, some striding over the ill man in their haste. But if they had time in hand, they paused to see what was wrong.

This experiment exposed a horrid truth: that kindness is situational. It explains the statistic that people living in fast-paced cities are the least helpful.

ESCAPE THE HURRY TRAP

Emotional wellbeing is not a steady state. You can elevate it. According to the British Government's 2008 Foresight project on Mental Capital and Wellbeing, which took contributions from over 400 psychologists, psychiatrists, neuroscientists, educators and economists around the world, there are five evidence-based actions that you can incorporate into daily life to improve your wellbeing:

> **Connect**
> **Be active**
> **Take notice**
> **Keep learning**
> **Give**

So what you might call moral behaviour – actions that promote social good – have been scientifically proven to be good for you. Stride purposefully through life, mind always bent on a goal, and you risk robbing yourself of a deeper purpose, and pleasure. All in all, it sounds like the sort of advice that Charles Dickens was trying to impart in the tale of miserly Ebenezer Scrooge in *A Christmas Carol*.

Unfortunately these wellbeing-promoting actions don't come automatically, the less so if you're hurrying or swamped by a time-poor, scarcity mentality. So here are some tips to make them easier:

- Build sociable, learning, generous activities into your routines.
- Hit the refresh button on friendships: make friend nights the new date night.

Slowing down isn't always viable. Reaching good, generous decisions under time pressure is toughest in business, where fast returns are seen as virtuous, and short-termism is in the ascendant. As James Gleick wrote in *Faster*, 'Silicon Valley venture capital firms are starting to seek fantastically short life-cycles for the companies they finance: eighteen months, they hope, from launch to public stock offering.' To avoid making bad

Hone your perspective-shifting skills, practising the art of mental time travel (see Lesson 20).

Next time you're late and stressed, remind yourself that your emotions will not speed you there any sooner. Try to take a moment to breathe, and be aware of your environment. Notice the flowers, the way the light falls. Savour it, and mentally check out of the panic zone.

Before a challenge, rummage in the memory bank. Can you summon an occasion when you triumphed over something equally daunting? Now project your mind ahead, visualize what success might look like. With a clear picture in mind, stress dissipates, success feels more inevitable, and your performance will improve.

choices under time pressure, you need to be proactive. Notice the triggers that stop you seeing the big picture, and have a protocol to compensate for them. Create a trapdoor to escape from the cognitive tunnel that hurry drives you into.

- The instant you feel the panic blinkers descend, step back. Ask: what is in your long-term interests? What does the broader horizon look like?
- If you regularly make high-pressure decisions, draw up a checklist of criteria to ensure all dimensions are considered. Who will be affected by this decision? What is the kind thing to do? How would your enterprise profit from promoting different values?

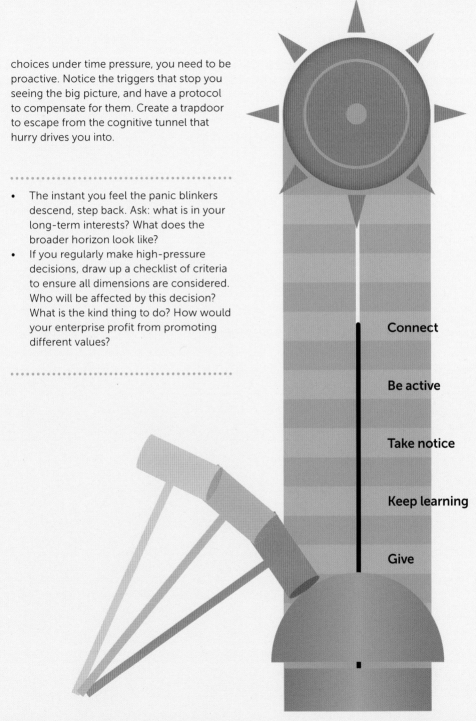

Connect

Be active

Take notice

Keep learning

Give

TOOLKIT

05

When time changes speed, this reflects changes in your environment, your perceptions and your emotions. Sometimes the clock slows to help you out of a tight spot. But when time drags, or seems too fast, take that as an instruction to change your situation or your emotions. Excitement and novelty make time flow faster yet render experience richer and more memorable. If you want to slow the clock, step back: dwell on details to savour the moment.

06

Your tempo echoes your emotions, but altering tempo can change how you feel. You automatically change pace to match the pace of your environment (entrainment), which can be handy but leaves you vulnerable to manipulation. So when muzak tickles your feet to march faster around the supermarket, or relaxing jazz induces you to linger over dinner and order another bottle, be aware and you can resist these pacemakers.

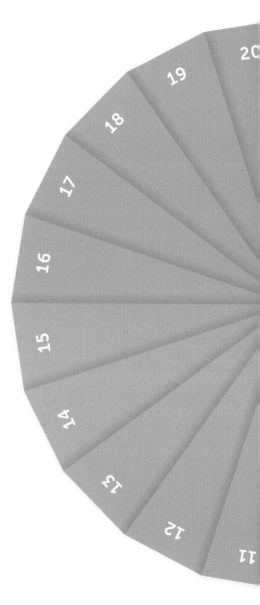

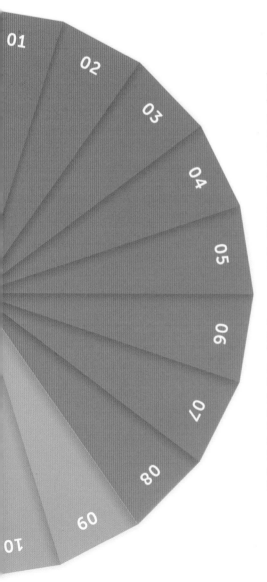

07

Distractibility helped our species conquer this planet. Now it enables social media to poke holes in your day, slowing you down, draining your mental energy and willpower. Worse still, dopamine addicts you to your smartphone, so interruption feels pleasurable. Wean yourself off social media, put it in quarantine, and use it as a reward for concentrating – at a set time, for a set number of minutes. Gradually it can help build your powers of concentration.

08

Hurrying raises the heart rate but lowers moral standards. Feel short of time and as your mind fixes on a goal, you can lose sight of the here and now as well as the bandwidth to be generous or take a long view. So if you must work fast, allow for these shortcomings. Slow down. Be kind, sociable and create space to breathe between tasks. Broadening your outlook will deepen your happiness.

FURTHER LEARNING

READ

Being Human
Richard Gross (Routledge, 2012)

Driven to Distraction at Work
Edward M. Hallowell (Harvard Business Review Press, 2015)

Thinking, Fast and Slow
Daniel Kahneman (Penguin, 2012)

The Marshmallow Test
Walter Mischel (Little Brown, 2014)

You Are the Music
Victoria Williamson (Icon Books, 2014)

Irresistible: The Rise of Addictive Technology and the Business of Keeping Us Hooked
Adam Alter (Penguin, 2017)

'Mental Capital and Wellbeing: Making the Most of Ourselves in the 21st Century'
www.gov.uk/government/collections/mental-capital-and-wellbeing#final-project-report

WATCH

Look at Me (Comme une image)
A brilliant multi-strand movie that dramatizes the pathos of distraction in family and relationships

Slowing Down Time (in writing & film)
Aaron Sitze, https://ed.ted.com/lessons/slowing-down-time-in-writing-film-aaron-sitze

DO

Forest App
An appealing app that rewards you for not picking up your phone.

WHY IS IT SO HARD TO ENJOY TIME?

LESSONS

Time is a puzzle, but understand how your beliefs about time shape your life and you can change the picture.

No time? Nonsense. You have more at your disposal than any previous generation. The average British woman's life expectancy is 83 years and increasing by 4 hours each day. The average British man's is 80 years and increasing at a rate of 6 hours per day, so he may catch up with women soon.

It's all very well knowing this. The burning question is, how do these extra hours in the future translate into more time for the here and now?

Most people believe the opposite: that time is shrinking, accelerating, ungenerous – despite all the machines to do our chores, all the technology to broaden our horizons, all the cheap travel, all our friends and likes on social media. And this is a pity, because it is impossible to overestimate the extent to which your experience of time is distorted by your expectations.

The following lessons explore the sometimes fabulous, sometimes insidious fashion in which your hidden beliefs about time shape your life, and why and how you might alter them. Time is a puzzle that has tickled philosophers for millennia, and if enjoying it can be a balancing act, organizing it is no picnic. Routinely we miscalculate time, and procrastination is rising. According to Professor Piers Steele, in 1978 5% of the population were chronic procrastinators. By 2007, this leapt to 26% – and that was before digital devices invaded our days and bored holes in our nights. But refresh your routines, massage your perspective on time, and you can do more than staunch the losses.

We should be ambitious about time, not fear it. If you are lucky, have good health and last those eight plus decades, you can expect 1,000 months on earth. What might happen if you saw your unfolding lifetime as a story told in 1,000 chapters? What if you decided to make each chapter interesting?

IS ENJOYING TIME EVEN POSSIBLE?

The earliest philosopher to argue that we should enjoy time was Epicurus. I've always been fond of him, not least because he opened the Garden, the first philosophical school in ancient Athens to regard women as worth admitting to its ranks, though some suspected him of less than worthy motives. The words emblazoned across his gate beckoned in passers-by, promising an exceedingly warm welcome: 'Stranger, here you will do well to tarry; here our highest good is pleasure.'

Do you picture a highbrow Hugh Hefner? In reality, Epicurus had more in common with Buddha than the lusty god Bacchus. He won a lascivious reputation because he championed a marvellously appealing theory: that good is found in pleasure and evil in pain. To him, a good life meant striving for bliss and avoiding sorrow; however, this did not make him the patron saint of partying. In his view, the apotheosis of pleasure was the absence of pain. Therefore to pursue sensual desires could be at odds with goodness, since overindulgence is inherently bad, and sensations like craving, wanting, needing are often painful too. Instead, ultimate bliss came of contentment, calm, an absence of fear of death: a life without time pressure, you might say.

Epicureanism's principles highlight three emotions that make time's passage less than smooth:
> Frustration
> Compulsion
> Dread

These emotions determine whether your hours feel free or circumscribed, expansive or parsimonious, fast, or slow, or hunted. If you're in their grip, escaping time – untethered by obligations, not a care in the world, never mind a worry for tomorrow – becomes highly attractive.

On the other hand, nobody could claim that life without time would be enjoyable. As a more recent philosopher, Immanuel Kant, observed in his *Critique of Pure Reason* (1781), time is 'at the foundation of all our intuitions'. It grounds reality and keeps us safe.

Try to imagine your life without time's compass. There are individuals, sufferers of a condition known as dyschronometria, who possess no inner mechanism for assessing duration (usually due to brain injuries). Consequently, they don't know when to stop talking, or how early to leave for work, or how many minutes to grill the toast before it catches fire, and their friendships, relationships and careers often buckle under the strain.

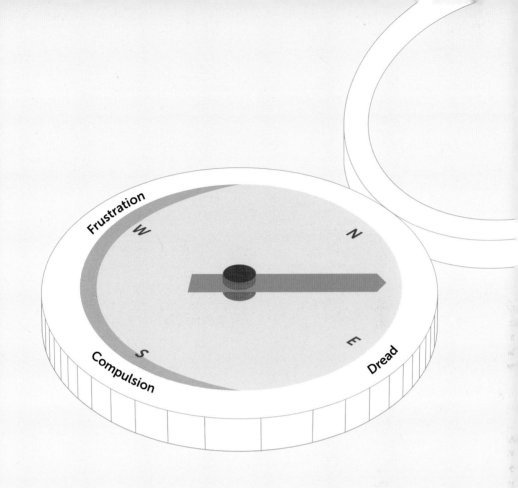

Dates and numbers don't just segment the sensory onrush of experience into manageable chunks. Time also performs an invaluable psychological service, imposing a form on terrifying existential uncertainties, such as duration and decay, as well as peculiar, abstract feelings, such as your sense of inevitability. It gives you a history, your identity, accumulating meanings – all your reasons to stay alive.

The flipside of these benefits is that time itself can resemble a cruel god. And generally, enjoying time means forgetting about it, and not just because it reminds you that you are mortal. You watch the clock when you long for a meeting to end, or fret about being late – rendering yourself less 'present', less 'in the moment', as the clichés have it. Catching a lover's eye on their wristwatch is the antithesis of an aphrodisiac.

But as all philosophers recognize, we need to think about time in order to live well. So how can you do that *and* enjoy it?

FINDING THE BALANCE

Time is the tightrope that tethers your journey between cradle and grave. To enjoy the trip is a question of balance: between the claims of today and the demands of tomorrow, between short-term pleasures and your long-term interests.

There are many varieties of pleasurable time. From epic sunny afternoons in which it seems abundant, endless, inconsequential, to ecstatic nights that pass in a giddy eye-blink. Likewise, lost in a task, you sink into that deliciously timeless, unselfconscious state known as 'flow' – so named by Mihaly Csikszentmihalyi, progenitor of the positive psychology movement, which is dedicated to refining strategies for happiness. Not feeling that we must think about, control or plan time – just feeling we have time – is liberating. Can you bring more of these kinds of time into your life?

The future does not excite everyone. Some would sooner face an empty plate than decide more than 30 minutes in advance what to eat for dinner. Perhaps numbers circled on calendars horrify you, or perhaps they thrill you; it depends on your mood and personality. But although there is no set recipe for how to enjoy time, it will not satisfy and nourish you without an element of agency. Reams of research show that if we don't feel our choices determine our actions, then our motivation, commitment and willpower shrivel. When you resent time – for being too fast, or too slow – what this reveals is that you aren't doing what you want. Living intentionally is the solution.

So stop dreading the calendar and clock. Remember that armed with time's measuring device you have an existential framework. You travel through each day with a direction. You get to weave the data flooding in through your eyes and ears and nerve endings into something more substantial: a tale of who you are and where you are going.

- Don't you wish you could revisit the thoughts of 15-year-old you? Wouldn't you like to tell that person everything will work out? Well, writing a journal offers similar reassurances, here and now. A diary entry doesn't need to be lengthy to change your perspective on life. Try a five-year diary. These ingenious books offer a page for each date of the year, with five brief entries per page, one entry for each day, so at the end of the year one, you begin the diary again, and as you write that second entry on the page, you re-encounter your thoughts from the previous year. It's compelling, often comforting.

- Just as knots on a string hold together beads of a necklace, so accomplishments are priceless marks in time. Celebrate big occasions, birthdays, anniversaries, as well as little turning points. Take time to reflect on how far you've come.

- Is your calendar on your smartphone? Go and buy a paper one and tack it to a wall you see every day. You're less likely to forget dates or to over-commit. You'll build anticipation too.

Keep a diary: not just a day-planner, but a proper journal. Reflecting on your day distils thoughts and feelings, puts life into proportion and broadens your perspective.

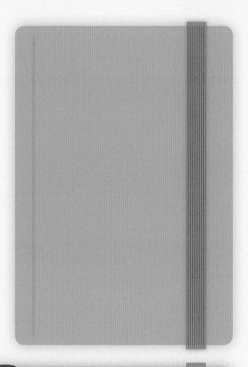

03 OCTOBER	04 OCTOBER
YEAR 1	YEAR 1
YEAR 2	YEAR 2
YEAR 3	YEAR 3
YEAR 4	YEAR 4
YEAR 5	YEAR 5

MISCALCULATING AND PROCRASTINATING

Most time-management guides will urge you to squeeze every last drop of productivity from your bitter lemons. I always feel weary reading them. Why must productivity be my ruler? Will my best ideas really bubble up in the brainstorming window scheduled to happen at some point between my first trip to the bathroom and my jog to the 6.05 a.m. to Liverpool station?

To me, the freedom to have time – as opposed to organizing it – is key to releasing potential, pleasure and creativity in a work-obsessed world. It fosters the slow, relaxed mood that is most fecund for creative, fresh ideas, according to the Nobel laureate Daniel Kahneman, in his bestseller *Thinking, Fast and Slow*. But I also recognize that gaining the freedom to be relaxed about time can be a battle. Most of us must work, and few dictate our working hours. And fundamentally, procrastination isn't relaxing either. Miscalculating the time needed to accomplish tasks not only undermines the quality of work, but the resulting stress can

poison what should be free hours.

It is common to underestimate the importance of time when deciding where to invest it. We're accustomed to making trade-offs. We place money before time, or we choose a larger, cheaper home in a remote location over a smaller one with a shorter journey to the office, kissing goodbye to morning and evening hours with people we love, instead spending them among strangers on a rammed train. Even those who should know better make this mistake, such as the commuting behavioural psychologist David Halpern, who confessed, 'We'd probably have been happier if we had spent the money and the time on doing something with [our children].'

Cleverness is no protection against misusing time. Robert Boice, Professor of Psychology at Stony Brook University, New York, spent six years studying the work practice of professional academics and identified six hallmarks of compulsive procrastinators:

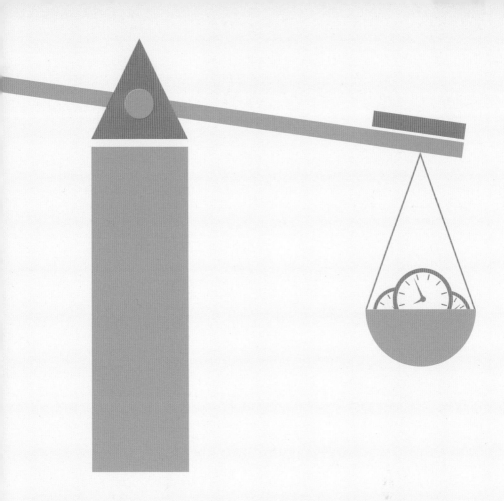

> Rushing
> Thinking more about product (quantity of
  work) than process (how it's produced)
> Anxiety (distractible, tense, fidgety)
> Unrealistic expectations about how to
  complete work
> Hostility to methods designed to impose
  structure or punctuality
> Poor results

Sound familiar? Well prepare to fight back.
And whatever you do, please don't call
yourself a procrastinator. The trouble with
labels is that they can be self-fulfilling,
because we feel compelled to act in
ways that conform to our self-image
(psychologists term this 'consistency bias').

So try not to quip, like the novelist
Douglas Adams, 'I love deadlines. I like the
whooshing sound they make as they fly
by.' Procrastination means putting things
off, even when you know it is against your
interests. On the other hand, well-managed
delay is essential to good time management.
So why not think of yourself as someone
learning to delay better?

TACKLING PROCRASTINATION

There are five reasons to procrastinate:
> Incapacity (not being up to the task)
> Situation (mess, disorder, poor planning)
> Arousal (you love the drama)
> Indecision
> Avoiding failure

To minimize them, be chary of taking on too much, and create conditions in which goals are more achievable. The more often you use time judiciously and stick to commitments, the more relaxed, realistic and reliable you will be.

As Robert Boice noted, chronic procrastinators consistently show poor judgement at calculating time for tasks. They justify this with claims such as 'I work better under pressure' (yes, we work under pressure; 'better' is a matter of opinion). One useful exercise is to list the reasons you fall back on to rationalize putting off work. Now ask yourself: are they self-defeating? Get wise to these excuses, and next time you hear yourself use one of them, override it. See it as a trigger switch to interrupt your habitual reaction and readjust your mindset.

Unfortunately, there are two unhelpful ways in which our minds warp time. First, the remoter a deadline, the likelier that we will underestimate a task's complexity, and therefore how long it will take to complete. Second, the more complicated a task – the more steps that it involves – then the further off the deadline seems.

Another issue is that temptations are horribly attractive. In a phenomenon called 'hyperbolic discounting', when offered the choice between £90 today and £99 tomorrow, usually we choose the former. If the choice becomes £90 in twenty days, but £99 in twenty-one, we pick the latter. Rational choices are easier when we take a long view, but an immediate temptation always appeals most: that hour watching television is invariably more attractive than an extra hour on a spreadsheet.

Taken together, these factors mean that instinctively we defer difficult things – often deceiving ourselves that there is still plenty of time.

To delay purposefully, train yourself to intercept the impulse to procrastinate. As soon as you notice it happen, stop. Ask yourself why you are deviating from your plan? What took your attention? Now examine the costs and benefits of delaying. If you remain convinced that deferral truly makes sense, identify a time when you will return to the task. Write down this new time and you will find it harder to defer when it comes.

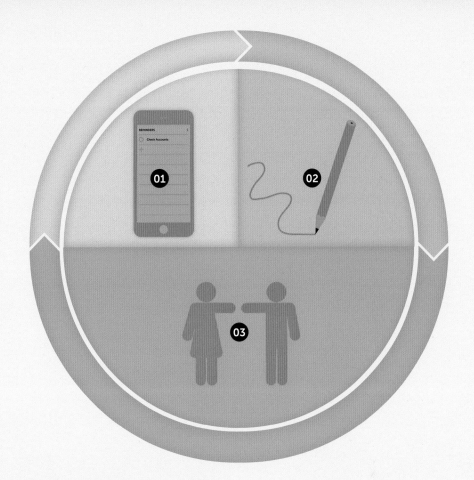

HOW TO COUNTER THESE WEAKNESSES?

01. Use pre-commitments. For example, arrange a regular monthly standing order to a savings account, giving the upper hand to your sensible, long-term, planner self – the part of you who has decided to save a deposit for a flat. Then you won't splurge all your salary in the sales. In the same way, book a regular spot in your schedule for that challenging project.

02. Plan in detail. Use step-by-step deadlines to crystallize what is realistic and necessary to complete a task. First break it into stages, calculating how long each will take, then allocate dates to begin and end each phase. Now write down the plan in ink – this deepens psychological commitment, studies find.

03. Share your plan with a friend, sending regular progress reports. Social pressure (i.e. embarrassment) is a great barrier against backsliding!

DON'T PROC

PRIORITIZE

PURPOSEFU

RASTINATE.
AND DELAY
LY.

WHY EVERYONE SEES TIME DIFFERENTLY

What does your attitude towards time reveal about you? Does it liberate or limit you?

These may strike you as mystical questions, but your beliefs about time aren't airy-fairy abstractions. Compelling research shows they are incredibly relevant, playing a huge yet easily overlooked role in steering your life.

Everyone has a different image of time. For instance, I picture it as a path, a bit like a ruler. Notches down its length represent hours, days, weeks, and as I move along it, my past stretches behind me, my future ahead. This concept of time feels logical and natural to me, but really it's just a metaphor, informed by the scientific age in which I live. Time looked very different to the elderly statesman-playwright Seneca

in 65 AD, a less scientific era. Sitting in exile at his country estate, awaiting an untimely death at the orders of his ex-boss, the mad Emperor Nero, he began composing letters to his friend, Lucilius, summing up his life philosophy. In letter twelve, 'On Old Age', he describes time as 'large circles enclosing smaller', with childhood at the centre, banded by youth then maturity. Sound strange? This image recalls the rings in a tree trunk. What metaphor could be more natural in rural Rome, where trees were more plentiful than rulers?

Time metaphors differ for different people, but our personal sense of time rarely adheres to rigid proportions. Some days are bigger than others, and the more significant an event, the nearer – and larger – its memory

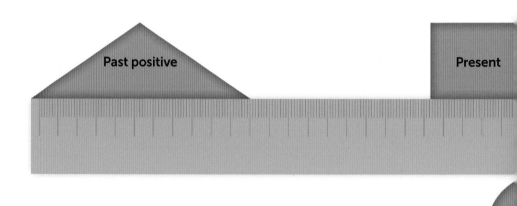

Past positive

Present

appears; a child's birth, for instance, always feels 'like yesterday' to the lady at the business end. This helps to explain why, for an older person, routine, unmemorable days glide by, whereas every day is an eternity to a little child, a treasure trove plum full of intriguing new information.

The psychologist Philip Zimbardo had a revolutionary idea: that some attitudes towards time are healthier than others. His name may be familiar. He ran the infamous 1971 Stanford Prison experiment, in which students played guards and inmates in a mock prison. Within three days the guards turned sadistic, the prisoners masochistic, and even the governor, one Philip Zimbardo, became sucked in. The study was abandoned, but its results made waves because they challenged notions of innate evil by showing that character is moulded by dynamic circumstance. This insight led Zimbardo to fresh avenues of study, until he discovered that our outlook on time – our sense of the past, disposition towards the future – is itself a dynamic force, steering us towards good and evil, joy and sorrow. From this he developed a new theory: the balanced time perspective.

Zimbardo would say a balanced time perspective is past positive (happy memories, fondness for traditions); present balanced (full of zest, believing that your actions will make a difference); and future positive (you make plans, expect things to get better). By contrast, an unbalanced perspective, particularly a fatalistic one, is often found in those suffering depression or low mood.

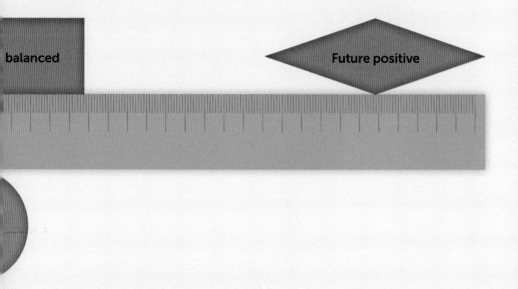

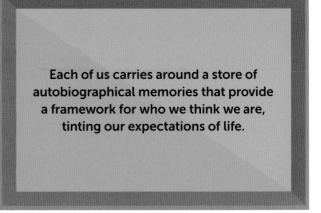

Each of us carries around a store of
autobiographical memories that provide
a framework for who we think we are,
tinting our expectations of life.

REBOOT YOUR PERSPECTIVE ON TIME

Few of us notice the extent to which our actions and expectations are infused and influenced by our beliefs about time. This is unsurprising, since these beliefs are scarcely visible. Yet what they do is filter our view of the world, rather like a pane of glass – glass composed of our perception of our past, present and future, and all the life lessons distilled over the years.

For instance, each of us possesses a store of touchstone autobiographical memories – the ones that you carry around like lucky coins in your pocket. These talismanic tales represent your ideas about who you are, so they shape your behaviour, helping to define whether you expect good or bad of life – whether you regard time as a generous benefactor, full of promise, or a blind force carelessly determining your fate, no matter how hard you strive. I daresay you wouldn't articulate it in quite these terms; probably you'd say you're a pessimist or optimist. But peel away these unhelpful labels and you can dismantle the assumptions that inform them.

Once you truly begin to notice that pane of glass and whether it is rose-tinted or dark, this opens the thrilling possibility that you could alter it, changing your perspective on life, how you react and act, catalyzing change for the better.

The evidence supports Zimbardo's claims. Future-oriented societies enjoy

LET'S TEST YOUR ATTITUDE TO TIME
01. What are your strongest memories?
02. How would you describe your feelings about the past?
03. What are you planning to do this weekend and why?
04. What does your future hold?
05. Examine your answers. What do they reveal about your attitude to the past, present and future?

greater economic success than the present-oriented. Future-oriented individuals have better impulse control, and the most effective people tend to entertain warm feelings about their past and future. What is more, people blessed with detailed memories are better at formulating plans and setting specific goals, demonstrating that having a firm handle on the past will help you lay firmer foundations for the future. It's a simple message. The greater your faith in your yesterdays and tomorrows, the happier your reality.

The good news is that you can rebalance your perspective. Working with individuals suffering post-traumatic stress and mental illness, Zimbardo developed a treatment plan that cultivated positive memories, by focusing his patients' attention on events when they felt loved and powerful. This mental shift helped them to become more active and optimistic in daily life.

You need not suffer trauma, or spend hours on a therapist's couch to shift your outlook on time. Small adjustments produce results, as shown in a study at Miami University. Researchers asked 300 students to recall an occasion when somebody hurt them. Afterwards they asked them to do some writing: one third were instructed to describe the event in detail, dwelling on their anger and sorrow; another third to describe it, then explore the good that flowed and what they learned from it; the remaining third described their plans for the next day. Afterwards, the second group were the most forgiving, and least likely to avoid the person who caused their pain.

Paul Dolan, author of *Happiness by Design*, argued: 'Being happier means allocating attention more efficiently; towards those things that bring us pleasure and purpose and away from those that generate pain and pointlessness.' So try to identify lessons in bad experiences, to cherish happy memories, to plan pleasures. Make these a habit and you will gain a healthier mindset about time, and your life.

LIVING ON AUTOPILOT

Life is habit forming. And those habits then have a nasty habit of taking control of you. 'People do not decide their futures, they decide their habits and their habits decide their futures,' as F.M. Alexander, who invented the Alexander Technique, wrote.

You may not feel as though you sleepwalk through your days, largely on autopilot, but almost certainly you do. It's estimated that habits constitute 40% of adult behaviour. An even greater proportion of your time is governed by mental rules of thumb – assumptions, beliefs – that guide your actions from one moment to the next (academics call these shortcuts 'heuristics').

Yet all of this is a mark of your sophistication. Mathematician Alfred North Whitehead pointed out that 'civilization advances by extending the number of operations we can perform without thinking about them'. Similarly, your unthinking habits serve to civilize your existence because they are remarkably efficient at automating behaviour. Not having to stop and cogitate about dull, regular but ineffably detailed physical actions lets you do things like run without tripping and eat without choking – freeing up extra cognitive capacity for your mind to wander elsewhere and daydream about what to watch next on Netflix, or to strategize ways to land that coveted job promotion.

Admittedly, if you let your days calcify into conga lines of habits, life can grow predictable. On the other hand, by reducing decision making, routines are extremely useful, shearing off potential points of friction. When you glide from action to action, habit to habit, then, provided that the actions and habits concerned are beneficial, this fluency reduces scope for you to veer off and do something impulsive or self-defeating, like procrastinate. For instance, choreographer Twyla Tharp always started her day by dressing in workout gear, then hailing a cab to her gym – leaving her no window of hesitation in which to wonder whether she really wanted to go, or wouldn't rather loll in bed, scoffing cheese on toast...

Making decisions is not a bad use of time. Free will is humanity's highest power, and exercising choice can be delightful, such as when out shopping. But as you

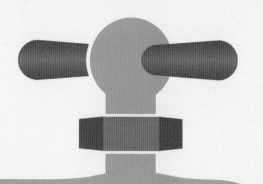

Time and energy leak unnoticed from badly planned routines.

pause to select between options, you slow down, and for every choice you make, something must be refused. It is a ripe breeding ground for anxiety and regrets about what you had to give up.

Go online and as your mental universe enlarges, your options multiply exponentially, at the risk of overstretching your decision-making apparatus. Search engines and price comparison websites supply not only bargains and data but abundant scope for stress, impulsivity and that frozen state, 'options paralysis'.

Become aware of your worst habits and you will begin to notice how insidiously they drain your time. But habits also thrive in a particular habitat. Change your environment, and they will too.

The danger of habits is that they neuter your engagement with life. Yet that is also their power: cultivate positive habits, live mindfully, tune your senses, and, uncluttered by unnecessary decisions, you can be an interested tourist moving through your world, attending to the things that good times are made of.

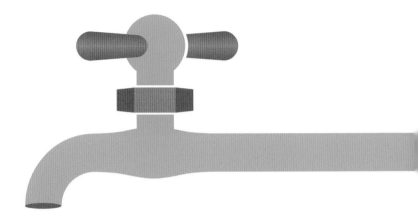

REFURBISH YOUR ROUTINE

In this universe of instant-access everything, a well-built routine can be your armour against self-defeating impulse and tedium. See it as a form of personal grooming: taking care of your time, improving its quality, will have the happy side-effect that both your self-image and your efficacy improve.

One useful way to think about your routine is as a gym instructor might think about a training session. The same rules for keeping workouts interesting apply to keeping your day interesting. Planning your schedule, it's important to factor in moments for spontaneity alongside necessary tasks. Yes it is a paradox, because serendipity is about happy accidents; nevertheless, carving out a dedicated space to be spontaneous means it is likelier to happen. Free time can even be scheduled for the same time slot each day. At school, they used to call it playtime.

Notice when your energy sags: this is your cue to rest or change gear. Bring in

contrasts too – vary the tempo, introduce moments of light and shade – and your routine gains depth. Seek out the golden moments in your day. Could there be more of them? Why not? And remember to mix things up periodically to avoid stagnation.

Weed out the things in your habitat that foster your bad habits. List the time thieves that regularly waylay and befuddle you, and examine your working environment with a critical eye. Is it messy or noisy? Is it just too easy to slide online, or raid the biscuit barrel, or to natter to Sue from accounts? Now put obstacles in the way of time wasting. Shut down the WiFi; put the biscuits on a higher shelf; block Sue's number.

Then clear the path to accomplish what really matters. Simple changes reap dividends. Tidy up. Make your workplace more attractive. Would a cushion help you sit longer? If you work in bursts timed by how long it takes to drink a coffee, invest in a bigger mug.

TRY THIS

01. Raise your consciousness of the unhelpful moments that litter your day. Where does time leak?

02. Identify your worst habits. What triggers them? How could you avoid these triggers?

03. Any kind of habit is hard to break. It is a lot easier to displace a bad one with something better. Once you have identified a quirk that you would like to stamp out, try grafting a beguiling new habit in its place. Make the new one fun, upping the element of novelty and contrast, to help it sink deeper roots.

TOOLKIT

09

Is enjoying time a paradox? We tend to be happiest when we forget the clock. Yet a successful life requires a balance: between the pleasures of today and the claims of tomorrow. Sometimes short-term delights conflict with our long-term interests. But appreciate time's importance as a tool and a comfort, note when you enjoy it, and you have a guide to using it better. Create carefree moments. Cherish good times. Lose yourself in activities.

10

Procrastination sells a false prospectus. It feels like you're buying time for fun, and life can seem more exciting, yet it sires poisonous guilt and produces substandard results. Everybody miscalculates the time needed for complicated projects. So plan better. Break tasks into step-by-step processes, assigning deadlines to each stage, and commit to the plan.

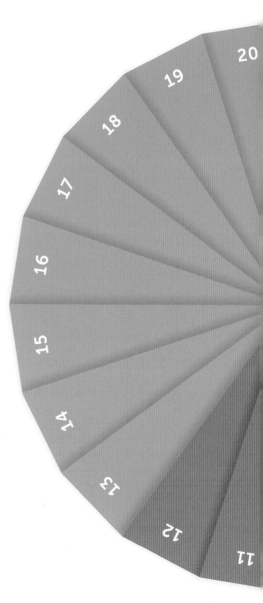

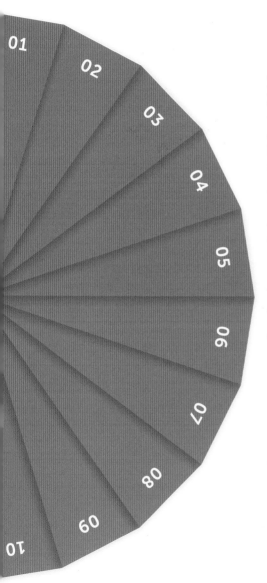

11

Your beliefs about time are like a pane of glass in your mind. You may not notice it, but it filters your outlook. Foster a positive perspective on time – happy memories; expect good of today and the future – and this can be self-fulfilling. But harbour toxic memories, feel your actions have no bearing on how life turns out, and this will shape your behaviour negatively, likely confirming your fears.

12

Habits can be your best friend or worst enemy. Some are treasured rituals; some automate behaviour, reducing time wasted on decisions. But inefficient habits throw obstacles in your path. Refurbish your routine to maximize the value of habits, making difficult things easier, and steering you away from drains. Change your habitat if need be. But don't let routine numb you to life's adventures. Carve space to be spontaneous, and keep varying the mix.

FURTHER LEARNING

READ

The Thief of Time
Chrisoula Andreou *et al*, eds. (OUP, 2010)

The Power of Habit
Charles Duhigg (William Heinemann, 2012)

Travels with Epicurus
Daniel Klein (Oneworld, 2013)

The Time Paradox
Philip Zimbardo and John Boyd (Rider, 2010)

WATCH

Dead Poets Society
Seize the day – and hit pause occasionally, to savour the poetry

Inside the Mind of a Master Procrastinator
Tim Urban
TED 2016

DO

Journal
Invest in a journal, perhaps a one-line-a-day, five-year memory book. Record, reflect and broaden your perspective.

STOP CHASING THE CLOCK

LESSONS

Does your life feel like a race against time? Or are you following your own beat?

Here is a time test. Next Wednesday, you and your best friend were meant to climb Everest/head for Vegas/visit a spa [delete according to preference]. But due to a scheduling clash, the date moved forward by two days. When will the trip take place?

Take a few seconds to think.

Did you answer Friday? Or Monday?

If the former, you have an ego-moving perspective on time: you see it as a track along which you run, heading to your future. If the latter, you have a time-moving perspective: you stand there, feeling as if time approaches you. These two perspectives seem to reflect opposed psychological dispositions.

I usually answer Monday, and feel disappointed: to me, ego-movers seem more like agents, in control of their lives. But there is nothing wrong with respecting time as an almighty force – so long as you do not feel like its victim.

If you answered the same as me, and worry that you have a passive view of time, you might be reassured to know that how people answer this question can change with their situation. Put this question to people waiting at a bus stop and they would be more likely to reply Monday. But ask them while they were jogging and more would answer Friday.

This little mind experiment reminds us that time is a perception, and that how you see it reveals a lot about you. Understand why you procrastinate, for instance, and you learn something about yourself that you might like to change. Do you faff because you crave drama or fear failure?

But time's compass is also a device for navigating life. The following lessons set out practical ways to navigate a smoother path through your day, drawing greater value from each hour, and setting your own pace.

LARK VERSUS OWL

The cliché that the early bird catches the worm continues to resonate. This is surprising, considering it is a concept born of a rural age, when we needed to finish work by dusk. Today technology lets us operate in multiple timezones if we wish. So why do we still hero-worship those up-at-dawn larks?

Morning people are often seen as high achievers. And funnily enough, high achievers talk loudest about their early starts. Chef, entrepreneur and father of five, Jamie Oliver, confided that he usually awoke at 4.45 a.m., tiptoeing off for half an hour in the bath. 'It's my only quiet time.' Next he headed for the gym, before (at a tardy 7.30 a.m.) beginning work, 'where time is planned to an inch of its life'. In other words, his morning routine was an act of escapology from an overly programmed day.

If you did not find US *Vogue* editor Anna Wintour impressive enough, then did you know that she packed in a blow dry and tennis match before clicking her Manolo heels to the office? Similarly, Condoleezza Rice, formerly a child prodigy pianist and ice skater, therefore used to forfeiting sleep for training, began her day as US Secretary of State at 5 a.m. on the treadmill.

In each of these cases, early time represents chosen time: time for not strictly essential things, outside work's rigid armature. But for other larks, an early start presents a golden time to work. Prolific

Victorian author Anthony Trollope paid his elderly groom £5 extra a year to bring him the cup of coffee that sped him to his desk by 5.30 a.m., where he scribbled for three hours, pocket watch in sight, to ensure he hit his target of 250 words every fifteen minutes – a technique that saw him finish over 24 novels as a full-time Post Office employee.

Trollope's regime wouldn't suit everyone. Night owls who claim they feel dead before noon are not fibbing. We all naturally incline to wake at a different hour, depending on what is called our chronotype.Early chronotypes rise earlier than late chronotypes. Although your genes dictate your chronotype and also the amount of sleep that you require, when you sleep is unconnected to how much sleep you need.

Chronobiologists attribute the wide variation between chronotypes to the fact that if left to our own devices, studies find, most people favour a sleep-wake cycle either longer or shorter than the solar day. As a result, pretty much everyone is in a constant minor state of jetlag, perpetually adjusting to conform with the 24-hour clock. Those of us who would naturally prefer a day shorter than 24 hours will wake earlier, and vice versa.

Research confirms an early start is common among successful people at the top of their tree. Does this mean night owls are doomed to languish at the bottom?

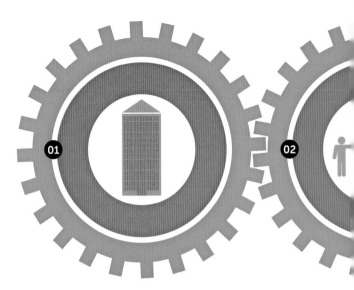

01

02

LEARN THE LARK'S TRICKS

Time management expert Laura Vanderkam explored what early risers accomplish while non-larks are still kissing the pillow and found they dedicate pre-breakfast hours to non-urgent matters that are personally important to them:

01. **Nurturing careers**
    (via strategizing or focused work)
02. **Nurturing family**
    (one-on-one time)
03. **Nurturing themselves**
    (exercise; pursuing a passion project)

This means that the benefits associated with early starts do not hinge on rising at a certain hour but on cudgelling space to indulge your priorities.

If you are not a natural lark, do not despair. Instead, seek to liberate your peak moments in time. You may believe that you do your best work after twilight, but studies conclude that in fact we are most alert, focused, logical and efficient three hours after waking. At this point levels of melatonin

(which makes you drowsy) drop, and serotonin and beta-endorphins kick in. This is an excellent time to devote to challenging work that demands intensive or original thinking. Another happy side-effect of these lively hours is that time seems fastest – great for spurring you on. So try to cherish the start of your day, whenever it begins.

It can seem easier to pursue priorities early in the morning, before the noisy world intervenes and other people start demanding your attention. But novelist Anne Rice successfully varied her work schedule throughout her career, toiling all night for her first book, *Interview with the Vampire*: 'I needed to be alone in the still of the night, without the phone, without friends calling, with my husband sound asleep.' After motherhood she reverted to a late morning start. To her, the hour itself mattered little; it was all about 'the uninterrupted three- or four-hour stretch'. You might be able to find that peace late in the morning – as babies sleep, when children are at school. It depends on your circumstances.

Your chronotype is not entirely fixed. For a start, it swings back and forth with age. As parents attest, young children are invariably larks, but come adolescence they wake later and later. Teenage girls' sleep-wake cycle begins to pendulum back to earlier waking 18 months before boys' – a difference that helps to explain why girls perform better in senior school exams. A poignant study found shifting the school day one hour later paid huge academic dividends for owlish boys.

So if you feel out of sync, you could nudge your chronotype. Try to adapt your environment and expectations, to be more sympathetic to your natural rhythms. Larks cull extra hours from the start of the day. Anybody can thrive by drawing extra value from their finest hours, whenever they fall.

PROTECT YOUR MORNING

01. To become an early bird, try changing your sleep cycle. Go to bed earlier and invest in a good alarm.
02. If you are always late, get up 15 minutes earlier.
03. Minimize choice and confusion: select clothes and other items the night before.
04. Minimize conflict: if fights about what to eat are the norm, agree a breakfast menu in advance.
05. Pick your battles: shouting may speed things up, but it also drains your resolve and morale.
06. Focus. No smartphones at the breakfast table please.

QUIT THE JUGGLE AND MONOTASK

You're in the shower, planning the presentation that you're due to give this afternoon. But you've barely run through your opening remarks before those intrusive thoughts come knocking: of the person you forgot to email that report to yesterday; of the invoice you must issue by 9 a.m.; of that outfit you must dry clean before Wednesday's conference – except today is Wednesday. . . You resolve to jump out of the shower, skip breakfast and start wrangling. You just need a pen and paper to write it all down. But by the time you find them – poof! – you can't recall a thing. Never mind, it will come back to you. And when it does, well, you'll just have to juggle.

These types of thought processes are a common response to overload. They are a warning sign that you are suffering from a mental state that has been dubbed 'popcorn brain' by organizational expert Carson Tate. It is what happens when a stressed mind can no longer process its cognitive load and begins flinging out ideas at random, only for them to vanish when you're in a position to do something about them. Very probably you're also practising that profoundly inefficient activity known as multitasking.

In general, juggling is seen as a virtue – particularly among working parents, who are praised for dashing about like an unrecognized branch of the emergency services. But although multitasking is arduous and skilful, does that make it something to be proud of?

'Switching from one task to another is effortful, especially under time pressure,' observed psychologist Daniel Kahneman. Given that with the invasion of digital technology, a semi-focused state of 'continuous partial attention' (coined in 1998 by writer Linda Stone) is increasingly the norm, arguably most of us engage in task switching, most of the time.

You might think that surely we can transcend these limitations. The human brain is a miracle of neurochemical engineering, the most complicated computational device in the known universe, and magnificently plastic – that is, able to adapt to any environment and winnow sense from multiple datastreams. On the other hand, everybody knows how challenging it is to pat your head while rubbing your tummy. Entertaining more than one train of thought at a time is harder still.

Wrench away your attention mid-flow to direct it elsewhere, and that abandoned train of thought will keep on running, albeit at a lesser velocity. This creates attention lag, which results in what is called a 'hangover effect'. Put simply, your mind continues to ruminate unconsciously on incomplete tasks on what psychologists term our 'default

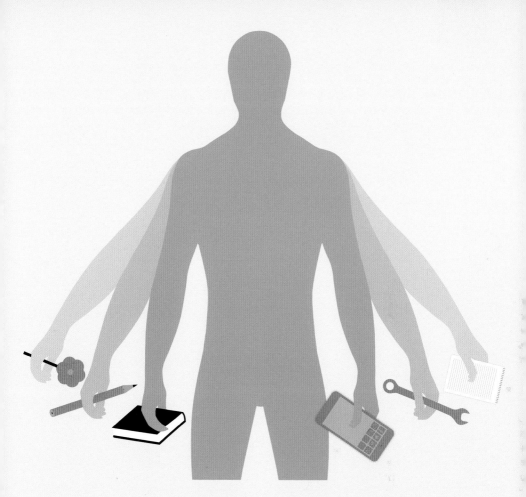

system'. This means that if you try to tackle a different task, your mental approach to it will be coloured by a cognitive hangover – all the thinking still quietly rumbling on regarding that previous incomplete task. This cognitive load can slow you down and stop you finding a fresh, appropriate method. What is more, hopping from task to task itself gives the illusion of time rushing faster, which is liable to drive your thinking into panicky cognitive tunnels.

Oddly, hangover effects persist only with incomplete tasks. Finish something and experiments find that your mind files it away, leaving no residue of rumination to colour your thinking for the next task. But the danger of whirling from task to task, leaving loose ends everywhere, is that your brain will keep those lines of thought open, waiting for you to return. When you consider how perforated your day is by bids on your attention – and how many of them burden you with a new task (if only to acknowledge an email) – then the stress must weigh heavy indeed.

THE JOY OF MONOTASKING

You may not regard multitasking as a choice. It seems pretty much mandatory if you operate in an open-plan office, or within reach of a smartphone, or a family, or a boss who likes sending emails.

But if you're tempted to do several jobs at once in the hope of speeding up, in reality you will slow yourself down. Tackling two jobs at a time takes 30% longer than one after another. You'll also make twice as many mistakes.

So why not quit the juggle? Monotasking means working in a linear fashion: one thing, then another. This is easier if you declutter your day. When planning the schedule, identify extended slots for focused work, also clearing space for contingencies (at the end of the morning, mid-afternoon, for instance).

Clear your desk, streamline your schedule, reassert that old-fashioned, linear style of working, put a higher value on your time, and you set your tempo. You will also end up with a tidier, calmer mind.

Interrupting used to be bad manners, but multitasking has become so commonplace that people come to expect it of us – at work, at home, even in our social life. They can even become insulted if we do not reply instantly. Though this has become normalized, it is possible to break with the norm. Lead by example, and train other people to respect the quality of your time.

- Responding immediately to an employer's demands may seem judicious, but lock into reactive cycles and you set a bad precedent, and can enter a working mode of firefighting – the opposite of that satisfying, forward-march feeling of making progress. So instead of doing what is asked straight away, send a holding reply, indicating when you will come back with an answer.
- If there are pressing issues and you cannot afford to go offline, timetable five minutes per hour to scan your inbox for emergencies.

Do not let that to-do list run away from you. Each evening write a list of all your goals for the next day. Once that day has begun, do not let a significant new item sneak onto the list to throw you off track.

If a new item crops up, note it, then set it aside. Unless it is a genuine emergency – in which case, deal with it in a contingency slot.

TO STOP R

MONOTASK

FASTEST T

PRODUCTIV

USHING,
IT'S THE
RACK TO
ITY.

DEADLINES NEED NOT BE DEATHLY

The Beatles are pop music's mightiest wonder. Trapped in a carnival of mass teen hysteria, and working pretty much eight days a week, as they famously sang, somehow the four lads from Liverpool held onto their sense of humour. More remarkable still, they kept pace with the treadmill for world domination devised by their manager Brian Epstein and record producer George Martin: one single every three months, two albums a year.

Most amazing is the quality of their output. 'The thing about the scale is that writing lots of songs is not particularly difficult. Volume is not the thing. The extraordinary thing about the Beatles is the amount of great songs,' said composer Howard Goodall, observing that Mozart was prolific, then Franz Schubert wrote about 800 songs – 'of which probably 100 are

absolutely beautiful melodies. Then you have to wait a pretty long time to get anyone up in the hundreds.' Until the Fab Four, who racked up 236 fantastic compositions in a decade.

How did they do it? In a stray hour, Paul McCartney and John Lennon would sit facing each other on twin beds in a hotel bedroom, acoustic guitars in hand. 'And we'd just start something and ricochet off each other.' They only wrote down lyrics, so had to remember the tune until they got into the studio. Which was painfully rare, complained George Martin.

But as far as McCartney was concerned, these limitations were an asset. 'One of the great things about our recording was the schedule. You'd go in at 10 o'clock in the morning, tune up, have a ciggie. . . then John and I mainly would present the song.' Then they had 'one and a half hours from

Deadlines can pave a faster path to creativity: locking you into a cognitive tunnel where your creative thoughts are harnessed.

10.30 to finish that song. Boom. So that focused you. That was a great discipline.' It proved a highly efficient pressure cooker for turning out perfectly formed pop.

The Beatles' madcap lifestyle recalls that of another young man trying to eke out a musical living, in Vienna two centuries earlier. 'It is impossible for me to describe the rush and bustle,' wrote Mozart's father during a traumatic visit to his son. He was not exaggerating. In 1782, a year he produced over 30 works, Mozart's daily schedule allowed him between 7 and 9 a.m. to compose, then between buttering up patrons and more lessons, he could not return to work until 'five or six o'clock in the evening, and even then I am often prevented by a concert. If I am not prevented I compose until nine.' After which he visited his beloved Constanze, returning to do more composition between eleven and one in the morning.

The triumphs of Mozart and the Beatles testify that deadlines aid creativity. True, they were not just working in those concentrated periods, but dreaming up melodies outside composing time, so being forced to work in snatched bursts let them ruminate constantly on incomplete melodies, and profit handsomely from their brain's default system (described in Lesson 14) – the unconscious part of your mind that broods on unfinished tasks while your conscious attention is elsewhere. Then when it came to committing their music to paper, time pressure locked them inside a fruitful cognitive tunnel – compelling them to be decisive, permitting no leisure to tinker or dither, moving them swiftly on from one work to the next.

FOCUSED TIME

TACTICAL DEADLINES TO UP YOUR PACE

Deadlines can open a faster route to glory. Their drawback is that if you panic, you may freeze or lose motivation and enthusiasm, or fall back on lower-quality, off-the-peg tactics rather than generating original ideas, custom-fit to the task in hand. So it is important to ensure that you have done the right preparation and brought the right tools for the task. Then when the pressure comes, deadlines can help keep you in a creative rather than an imagination-clenching tunnel.

When we are reminded that every second is irretrievable, it is easier to make every action count. So if you have a very narrow window in which to achieve a goal, try working in brief, focused bursts, setting a timer to go off every 25 minutes (the so-called Pomodoro Technique, named by its deviser Francesco Cirillo after a kitsch red plastic tomato kitchen timer that he owned

as a student). Maintaining tightly focused attention for longer than 25 minutes is tricky, but after a brief break, you can reset that timer, sustaining the cycle for up to 4 hours. Or imitate the early-bird novelist Anthony Trollope, who preferred to sprint through work in 15-minute bursts, 3 hours at a time.

Systematic time pressure can not only accelerate but also improve decision making. A Stanford University study discovered that strategic business decisions in microcomputer companies were of the highest quality not in those that took their time but in those that reached decisions most rapidly. This result seemed surprising, but in fact it reflected their organized approach. The top performers used more information to reach decisions than slow decision-makers, and generated a broader range of propositions before analyzing

01 Brainstorm

02 Focus

tactical plans for executing them. The most effective of all were those who ruthlessly reduced the number of decisions that they made, focusing their efforts on where they could gain the most. In other words, they were strategic about how they approached their strategy. They prove that sometimes less time really does produce more.

The more deadlines that you introduce into long-term or large-scale projects, the more targeted your efforts will be. Distribute time pressure as evenly as possible, not only breaking a task into step-by-step phases, but setting a deadline for each. For example, it's little use vaguely wanting to get fit. Instead, attach this objective to a specific challenge and date – say, to run 5K in under 30 minutes by 1 January – then, each day of training, set a new target to exceed your last.

Putting yourself in charge of your time pressures means that you cease to be that cowering person, facing a looming deadline. By cutting deadlines down to a manageable size, you up your confidence, will and ability to succeed.

HOW TO DECIDE FASTER
A good three-point plan for improved, rapid decisions is to:

01. **Brainstorm**
    (allowing a limited time for it)
02. **Focus on the relevant data**
    (have a checklist)
03. **Rate your options according to whether they meet your broader goals**

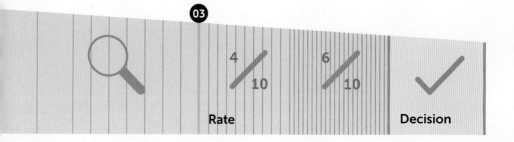

HARNESSING MOMENTUM

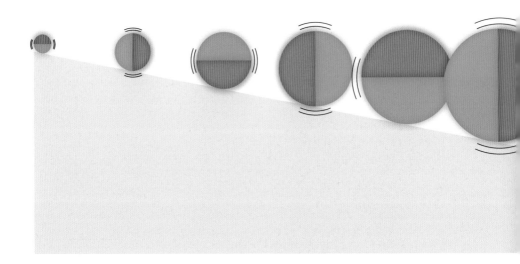

Today is absolutely the day to ask your boss for a raise, or tell your mother you can't stay two weeks over the holidays. You can't put it off another second. But before you do, you'd better check your emails. . . And it's hard to focus with an untidy desk. . . Is it lunchtime already! Better not call now, people aren't receptive to difficult conversations when they're hungry. . . Oops! It's wine o'clock. Best wait until tomorrow. . .

Everybody knows that tomorrow never comes. Yet it is always tempting to put present comfort (not doing the hard thing) before present discomfort (cracking on and doing it). Sadly, dealing with challenges also grows harder as the day goes by.

'Major self-control failures and other bad decisions occur late in the day,' observed willpower expert Professor Roy Baumeister. 'Diets are broken in the evening, not the morning.' This gradual weakening of will is ascribed to a phenomenon known as 'ego-depletion'. In essence, this means that to compel ourselves to do anything unappealing (or resist a temptation) we must draw on the reserves of our conscious self. Expending this effort leaves us less willpower for the next challenge.

Operationally, willpower is like a muscle: as its might fades, so does your ability to stick at things. To get more out of it, you need to train it. But although you can build up your capacity for sustained application, it is also wise to be sparing, conserving willpower for stuff that really matters. Eating a tempting treat can even help you to persevere at a demanding activity, one Baumeister study found, either because the reward restores willpower or because effort has not been squandered on resisting the snack.

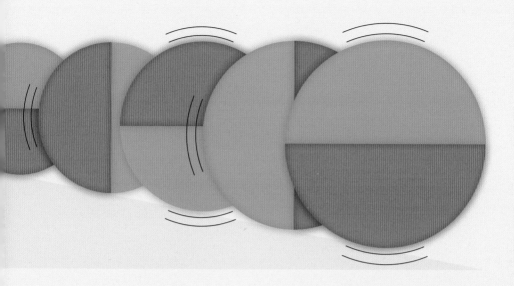

Although willpower's strength fluctuates, you can reap more from your efforts at different times. 'The first hour is the rudder of the day,' wrote the American preacher, Henry Ward Beecher. He meant that it sets the tone. Begin each morning in a whirligig of chaos, yelling about mislaid keys or burned toast, and your stock of good intentions is decaying before you leave home. But apply a gentle, positive pressure to the rudder and the effect on morale is equivalent to consuming a hearty breakfast, supplying motivation for greater challenges. The momentum of your day starts positively.

It is easy to underestimate momentum's relevance. Although it is a well-known concept, it is less well understood. The rules are clearest in physics, which defines momentum as the force of an object's movement: the heavier an object, the faster it moves, the mightier its momentum, and the trickier it is to stop or divert in a new direction. There are three ways to maximize momentum: increase the object's mass, increase its velocity, or reduce the friction and obstacles dragging against it.

The laws of physics translate well to psychological momentum. For instance, if I say that all the momentum in a tennis match is with Roger Federer, I'm describing a perception: my favourite appears to be heading for victory. And although each point is played in isolation, tennis is a mental battle; if Federer's opponent drops point after point, his hope and his concentration will fade.

Fundamentally, this is true for all of us. If you can conjure the sensation that you are charging purposefully towards your goal, your pace will pick up.

What reboots your willpowe

MORE POWER FROM LESS EFFORT

How can you harness momentum to spur on your day?

In the morning, when willpower peaks, hit the ground running, kicking off your day with a sense of accomplishment. An action as insignificant as tooth-flossing or making your bed is a keystone habit – one that, according to research, possesses an uncanny knack of triggering positive change in entirely unrelated areas of your life. Why? Small, orderly acts prime your mind with positive expectations.

Be mindful of what what reboots your willpower, and what depletes it. Can you do more of the former, fewer of the latter? And explore how your daily routine could be more exciting.

SIX WAYS YOUR ROUTINE CAN BOOST YOUR PACE

01. Set challenges: each week, find a new way to do a routine task.
02. Exercise at lunchtime to invigorate your afternoon.
03. Which regular events drag at morale? For example, that dispiriting walk through the subway passage past the graffiti may be a shortcut but it exacts a toll.
04. Allocate bitty jobs to tired hours, e.g. afternoons.
05. Take a break: to repair willpower and concentration.
06. We are social animals, and companionship nourishes us like food. So when you eat, try to do it with someone you enjoy spending time with.

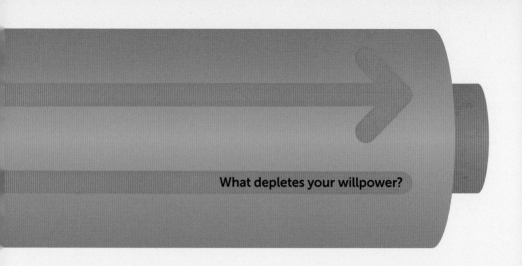

Train your awareness and you will find momentum drags are rife in the workplace. The greatest are meetings, which on average consume up to a third of the working day. They are too frequent, often with too many attendees, and too rare is the focused agenda and cracking chairperson to whip along proceedings. Worse, they divert us from the deep thinking that produces work of greatest worth. The solution is to limit meetings and keep them relevant.

There are several types of meeting, but not all are necessary.

> **Sharing information or instructions**
  Often pointless. Why not disseminate data online or by email?
> **Team building**
  Schedule these for the day's end, to protect productive hours, or bring back the communal lunch, the best networking forum.
> **Brainstorming, decision-making and problem-solving meetings**
  To keep these on point, circulate materials in advance, and meet in the morning, when our brain fizzes fastest.

'Walk out of a meeting or drop off a call as soon as it is obvious you aren't adding value,' advised Elon Musk, billionaire founder of Tesla – possibly easier if you are the boss. But we need to think harder about meetings in terms of meaningful value rather than as performance displays. One wonders how many would be axed if more companies used the *Harvard Business Review*'s business-meeting-cost calculator to rate the expense of attendees' salaries, then deducted it from the relevant department's budget.

- Beforehand, think: is this meeting necessary? Is my presence vital?
- Ensure the agenda is clear.
- Curb the chitchat.
- Ask what you could gain from a fresh approach. It is rumoured that Coca-Cola conducts meetings standing up, to keep attendees focused. Other companies meet in cold rooms. Could banishing smartphones achieve similar effects?

TOOLKIT

13

If you are one of the 1 to 3% of people, like Madonna and Leonardo da Vinci, who can survive on a few hours' sleep, this does not mean you are a morning person. But if you are a natural lark, use those quiet first hours for improving wellbeing or pursuing personal goals. If you naturally wake up late, create space for prioritizing your highest wants, and protect your peak stretches of time – especially the one that begins three hours after waking.

14

We lose masses of mental energy and time when we do too much at once. So clear the decks and monotask. You will find that a linear, sequential way of working unclutters your mind and is most effective. Avoid reactive cycles, training others to value your time as much as you do. Instead, assign tasks to specific times, setting aside contingency slots for overruns and genuine emergencies.

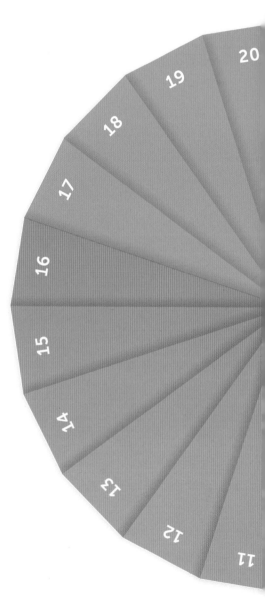

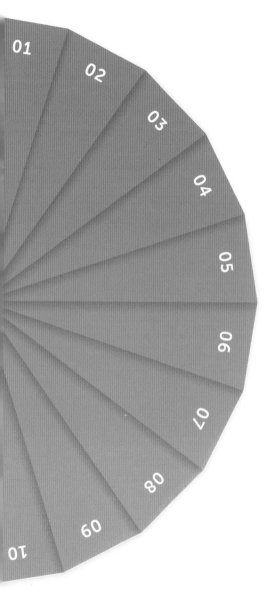

15

If the Beatles had had more spare time, arguably they would not have produced so many classic hits. Their genius demonstrates that although deadlines can be the bane of your life, used judiciously they put you in charge of your time pressures. To spread the pressure use step-by-step deadlines, put in the correct preparation, match the task with your skills, and deadlines will drive you into a creative and fruitful cognitive tunnel.

16

Willpower is a delicate beast; the harder you work it, the sooner it fades. But structure your day to build momentum and success can help to breed success. Start positively, tackling compelling and complicated work in the morning, to brew a sense of accomplishment. To minimize momentum drains in the workplace, reduce the number of meetings, the number of people attending, and banish distractions and chitchat, adopting a tight agenda and no-smartphones rule.

FURTHER LEARNING

READ

Willpower
Roy Baumeister and John Tierney
(Penguin, 2012)

Happiness By Design
Paul Dolan (Penguin, 2014)

Grit: The Power of Passion and Perseverance
Angela Duckworth (Vermilion, 2016)

Morning: How to Make Time. A Manifesto
Allan Jenkins (Fourth Estate, 2018)

The Craftsman
Richard Sennett (Penguin, 2009)

Work Simply
Carson Tate (Portfolio Penguin, 2015)

WATCH

The Beatles: Eight Days a Week
A stupendous and inspiring film about the Beatles, assembled from archive footage and interviews, old and new.

DO

Work on self-forgiveness
Science suggests that regrets deplete willpower. So, do not get upset when you miss the deadline. Be compassionate to yourself, draw up a new plan, and you are less likely to procrastinate tomorrow.

GIVE YOUR TIME MACHINE A NEW PROPELLER

LESSONS

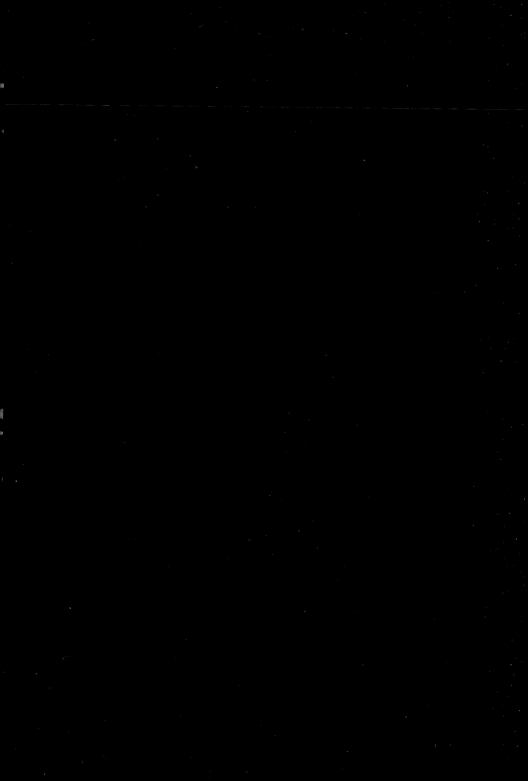

Believe that every minute must earn its keep and you do not just commodify your time: you also objectify yourself.

Say that we have a problem with time and usually we mean that we do not get enough done. But our fixation with productivity can be self-defeating.

This chapter explores why we should challenge the binary notion that life divides into hard-working, non-fun time, and unproductive, indulgent time might be self-defeating. It turns out that our grasp of which activities replenish and relax us is often misguided. Much as you may relish ogling screens, from surfing the Net to devouring Netflix serials, your brain cannot compute frictionless experience. This is why in sedentary, visual activity, time seems to evaporate; it is awfully thin existential gruel compared with the experience of previous generations, who lived primarily through their five senses, so were more attuned to their environment and, perhaps, to one another.

As we shift towards a culture in which increasing stretches of our lives are occupied in solitary, non-physical activity, and as anxiety and loneliness soar, prioritizing pleasure and connection are vital. Lesson 18 will cheer up productivity fans: all the evidence about what motivates us points to the fact that pleasure and a sense of ownership are key to perform effectively. Lessons 17 and 19 look at how to restore your senses and engagement.

Think of yourself as a time machine, motoring through life. To achieve long-haul ambitions you need grit. Make pleasure, passion and perseverance your propeller, then map the course to your destination. Time will grow richer and you will have more fun – and almost certainly get more done.

STOP TO GET MORE DONE

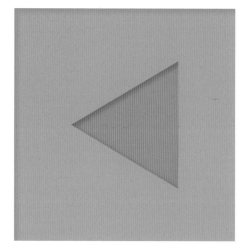

On 7 March AD 321, Emperor Constantine the Great issued a decree whose effects continue to shape your week. Henceforth, he proclaimed, Dies Solis, 'the day of the sun', would be a universal day of rest.

Rest may salve the soul, but it is no longer exactly sacred. Sunday closing is a distant memory, and once routine breaks in the day – lunch time, afternoon tea, going home time – are crowded out by work and distractions. In 2017, Reed Hastings, CEO of Netflix, a global business of a scale not much less influential than the Roman Empire under Constantine, declared that his company's main rival was neither Amazon nor YouTube, but sleep.

Chew on that thought and get angry. Because Reed's agenda is shared by the most powerful new global businesses. The great time heist is at full pelt. First they wanted your waking hours. Now they want your sleep.

We need rest, not just physically but psychologically. Human beings understand ourselves through memorable actions and events, experiences we share through stories. But if life is to be a tale worth telling, then you need to pause and break up your day, because the more distinct your experiences, the broader and deeper your perspective.

This is easier said than done. If you spend all day chasing to-do lists, it may seem wise to keep going until you've checked off the last damned item. And being lost in an activity can be delightful. When I glance up to see almost an hour has passed in what seems ten minutes, this is a sign that work is going well. All the same, stay glued to my chair for too long and after a certain point,

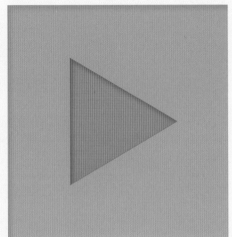

without me always noticing, my mind turns to mush.

This is why we should celebrate the pause, which is the Cinderella of time management – often overlooked, but incredibly hard-working and productive.

Researchers at Ben-Gurion University, Israel, demonstrated the importance of breaks when they analyzed the decisions of eight Israeli parole-board judges over a ten-month period and a shockingly consistent pattern emerged. At the start of the day, two-thirds of parole applications were granted. This number plunged almost to zero by the time the judges stopped for their first food break. No matter what offence the convict before them had perpetrated, if the judges were peckish and grumpy, they had no difficulty in summoning blistering legal arguments for keeping him behind bars. But after eating, their blood-sugar levels restored, evidently the judges were in a better temper, because they approved almost as many applications as at the day's start – only for this rate to slide once again until they stopped for their next bite.

This evidence is distressing for anyone who would like to believe that reason governs our actions. If distinguished professionals are so erratic, what hope have we?

I think that is the wrong lesson to draw from the data. For me, it underscores that your capacity to pay attention is contingent on time and wellbeing. Remember Lesson 16: your willpower weakens over the day. But a pause, snack or exercise repairs it, improving your decision-making apparatus too.

So put a premium on unpressurized moments. Or you can expect that rapacious to-do list to metastasize.

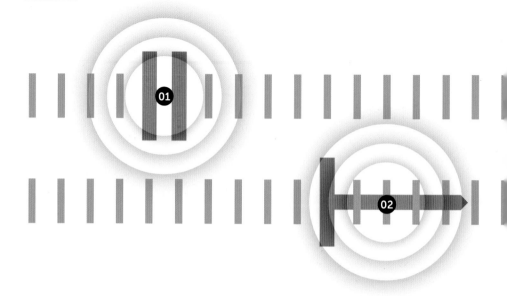

WHEN ARE YOUR CINDERELLA MOMENTS?

Breaks not only blow away the cobwebs, they also place a frame around time. So when you start the morning aware that at noon you must down tools to walk the dog, for instance, immediately the minutes within that timeframe gain urgency and value. This sense of structure drives you on.

Don't underestimate the usefulness of the pauses themselves. That idle three minutes waiting for a kettle to boil opens a quiet pocket in which your mind can relax enough to fling out elusive answers. How often have you broken off from a difficult task to go for a run or rinse the dishes, only to have a bright idea to bubble up when you were not looking for it? These happy inspirations feel serendipitous, but are produced by the dogged efforts of your brain's default system, working overtime on an incomplete problem. For this reason, many great artists

and thinkers swore by a daily constitutional walk, from Thomas Hobbes to Beethoven, Kant to Einstein. After a morning composing then eating lunch, routine-obsessed Russian composer Tchaikovsky often stumbled across new melodies during long hikes through the countryside, a notebook perpetually tucked into his jacket, just in case.

Comb through your routine and identify neglected Cinderella moments. Ask yourself:

01. What is your favourite pause switch for shifting pace?

02. When do you transition from one phase to the next?

03. Where are the natural breaks?

04. Are there enough calm moments, or do you jam them with activities?

05. Could you make more of these punctuation points to reset your mood and motivation?

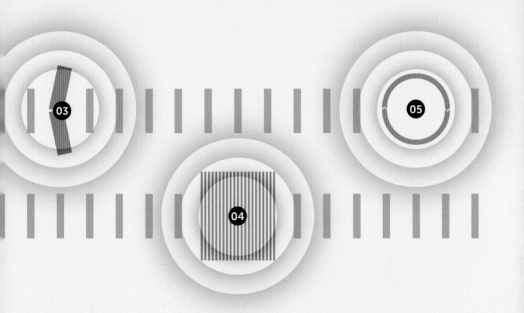

While we sleep, our brain consolidates learning, laying it down in our long-term memory (another reason to sleep well, particularly before an exam). So when in doubt or facing a problem, take a nap. If that is not possible, find a quiet spot where you can rest with your eyes shut. Or emulate the remarkable deaf mathematician, Dame Kathleen Ollerenshaw. When facing an intractable equation, she would write it on a slip of paper then pop it under her pillow at bedtime. Invariably she awoke the next day with a solution.

So shine a spotlight on the little rituals that shift your gear. Do them daily. Make them sacred. Rule out nothing. Sitting naked and taking a morning 'air bath' worked wonders for the statesman and thinker Benjamin Franklin. Painter Joan Miró kept depression at bay with daily bouts of boxing. Composer Shostakovich played football with friends and never missed a party, or a deadline.

Seek ways to make life feel simpler. A good friend of mine always had a frenetic morning exit, trying to get multiple persons, large and small, dressed, fed and out the front door, before doing the same for herself. On the way to work she always stopped for ten minutes to read in a coffee shop. She would read anything, but the rule was that it could not relate to work. This change of pace, reasserting her ownership of her time, was, she said, essential to her mental health.

WHY PLEASURE MAKES YOU WORK HARDER

What do I want to do today?

I doubt this is the first question on your lips when you wake up. Most of us are chivvied through the day by duties – needs, not wants. But how much easier might it be to spring out of bed if work felt more like a hobby?

A prime exponent of the work-as-fun philosophy was the writer Patricia Highsmith, who had a stupendously slatternly ritual for gestating a mood conducive to work: chainsmoking in bed, curled up like a baby, accompanied by a doughnut, coffee mug and more cigarettes, until the urge to scribble grew irresistible. She called this creating a 'womb of her own' – punning on Virginia Woolf's famous dictum that every female writer needed a 'room of her own'.

Despite these languid appearances, for Highsmith work was deadly serious, her life's core preoccupation. But her pseudo-casual approach to it reveals her shrewd grasp of human motivation. Although her tactics might not be your idea of fun, and would not satisfy any workplace health and safety directives, they succeeded in tickling her into a playful, non-pressured state of mind. And because work felt voluntary, less willpower was necessary to get going. Her

time and ideas felt freer as a result.

How could you remake work to resemble a hobby? Well, what does a hobby look like? Spending unending hours staring at water, waiting for a fishing rod to twitch may be your idea of heaven, but would be hell for me. And that is the point: a hobby can consist of anything you want. Bricklaying did it for Winston Churchill. The only salient characteristic that unites the many disparate, crazy, boring leisure pastimes people pursue is the fact that we choose to do them. Some also bring incidental benefits, such as an enriched social life with fellow enthusiasts, but hobbies' chief reward is fun. They are autotelic tasks, joyous ends in themselves.

A quick way to spoil a hobby might be to reward yourself for doing it. As Daniel Pink points out in *Drive*, his masterly book on motivation, every type of secondary incentive – from a threatened penalty for failure to a stonking great performance-related bonus – has one instant effect: it transforms an activity that could be play into work. Why? Because rewards, bribes and threats all transmit a subtle, unmistakable message: this thing that you're doing is only worthwhile because you're being rewarded/bribed/threatened.

The guiding argument of this book is that we should enjoy time instead of obsessing about productivity. So it might appear suspiciously convenient to claim that pleasure heightens productivity. It also goes against the grain of our capitalist economy, which is built on a very different motivational basis: the carrot-and-stick compensation culture. This may be why, despite mounting evidence, it took psychologists decades to accept that everything we believed about motivation is wrong, until a 1999 study analyzed 128 experiments and concluded: 'Tangible rewards tend to have a substantially negative effect on intrinsic motivation.'

Take note all parents who want children to do homework without being nagged. The instant that you introduce a work-and-reward structure (i.e. a coercive, extrinsic incentive), you leach a task of its intrinsic appeal, depleting the very motivation that you want to increase. Yes, promised lollipops help us to stick at a task in the short run, but in the long term they neuter our ability to delight in it. And if they encourage us to fixate on how long it will take to finish and get our hands on that lolly, then time will seem slow and dull indeed.

Being rewarded turns a pleasure into a chore.

REFRAMING WORK, FIRING MOTIVATION

If the essential attribute of a hobby is that there is no reward, how could your job seem more like one? Give up your salary? Not likely.

You could try to frame work differently, however, by enhancing its key motivating factors: autonomy, ownership, creativity.

- First – the simplest idea, but perhaps trickiest to put into practice – is to want to do what you're doing. If 'what we feel, what we wish, and what we think are in harmony', it is easier to slip into that delicious, time-forgetting state of optimal work effectiveness known as 'flow', according to Mihaly Csikszentmihalyi, who first identified this highly productive mental state. So be choosier about the work you take on. Consider how it chimes with your goals, interests and values. If it does not, could you align it more closely with your priorities?

- Second, design tasks to heighten your sense of ownership. If you have a strong 'internal locus of control' – that is, feel your actions determine your destiny – you tend to be more self-motivated and grittier. Soldiers perform best when they are empowered to decide how to achieve objectives. So if you work for a morale-trampling, sergeant-major type micromanager, manage up: present the route to their preferred solution, but try to devise as much of that route as possible.

01

Clear goals

Interrogate the negative effect of rewards and it becomes clearer that the problem is they neuter our sense of volition. They can also make us frightened of missing out or failing, which inhibits enthusiasm, risk-taking and creativity. For example, a study at Bing nursery in Stanford University discovered that when little children are drawing, they are inventive if it is for fun. But tell them they'll receive a Good Player Award card and a gold star and both their drawings and enthusiasm lose verve – they grow scared of not meeting the required standard. Similar results were produced in studies of adults doing mathematics puzzles, whose performance and persistence were greater when they just thought they were just messing around.

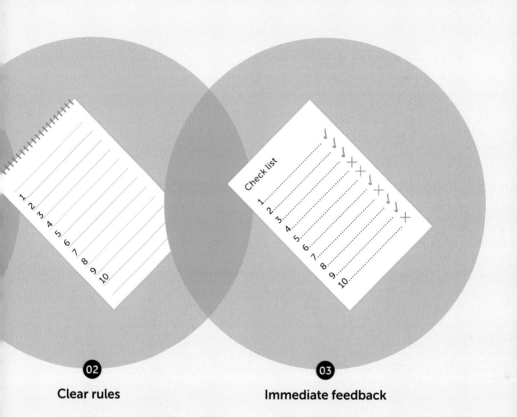

02

Clear rules

03

Immediate feedback

DESIGN WORK TO BE FLOW-FRIENDLY
We enter flow when we pursue an
activity at a level slightly beyond our
abilities, with the consequence that we
stretch and therefore improve our skills,
engaging us more deeply with what
we are doing. To make work feel more
like a flow-inducing game, you need:

01. Clear goals
02. Clear rules (measures of success
    and failure)
03. Immediate feedback (ways of
    judging whether you have met the
    required standard)

LIVE INTEN
LET DAILY
LEAD TO LC
GOALS.

TIONALLY.
CHOICES
NG-TERM

ALL RIGHT NOW

PAST

In April 1844 Henry David Thoreau and a friend accidentally started a fire that burned down 300 acres of Walden Woods, Massachusetts. This disaster lit the fuse for this restless man of letters to reappraise his life, and the following year he built a log cabin in the forest and withdrew there alone to 'live deliberately' for two years. He shared his findings in a book, *Walden*.

You must live in the present, launch yourself on every wave, find your eternity in each moment. Fools stand on their island of opportunities and look toward another land. There is no other land; there is no other life but this.

I dare say you have too much going on to disappear into the woods to meditate on existence. Yet it is all too easy to lose sight of the fact that each day is a stream of fugitive presents, moments that become irretrievable the instant they are lived. Frankly, it can be comforting to lose sight of it. Dream of your future, muse on your past, and it is possible to imagine our existence, like our gadgets, comes with a rewind and fast-forward button. Whereas if you believe

that we live only in the present then life seems short indeed. Approximately three seconds long in fact — the duration of what neuroscientist Ernst Pöppel defined as the 'window of the subjective present'.

Three seconds is how long your conscious mind can host a rich, detailed awareness of what is happening around you before this window closes and your short-term memory refocuses on a new present. At this point 'now' is irrevocably in the past, and your brain either files its details in your long-term memory, or more usually, it discards them.

Arguably, forgetting the incandescent riches of each instant is the kindest trick that your brain plays on you. How would you cope if it retained every detail? On the other hand, being able to sink into your present brings countless benefits.

Human beings do not naturally pay close, singular attention. While other animals concentrate on the here and now, our propensity to mind-wanderlust means that 46.9% of the time our thoughts are not on what we are doing. This statistic emerged from a 2010 study conducted by Harvard University psychologists Matthew

NOW

FUTURE

Killingsworth and Daniel Gilbert, who used an iPhone app to discover the real-time thoughts and feelings of 2,250 volunteers, asking at random intervals how happy they were, what they were doing and what they were thinking about. Gathering 250,000 data points, they concluded that although our hither-thitherness of thought is useful – and a deciding factor in our species' success – paying attention is critical to wellbeing. 'A human mind is a wandering mind, and a wandering mind is an unhappy mind. The ability to think about what is not happening is a cognitive achievement that comes at an emotional cost.'

They discovered something shocking: that we feel happiest not when we are doing particular things, or even thinking about happy things, but when our mind is on what we are doing. The implications are profound. What this means is that lying on a sunbed on a paradise island is probably less enjoyable than ironing, which requires your attention. This would explain why absorbing tasks such as cooking, crafts, sport and playing games are so satisfying. It also makes sense of why the practice known as mindfulness has become wildly popular.

HOW TO BE IN THE MOMENT

According to the World Health Organization, by 2030 mental health will be the biggest cause of burden (their term for lost or compromised years of life) of any illness in the world. Luckily we all have tools to improve our emotional habitat.

Professor Jon Kabat-Zinn, founder of the Stress Reduction Clinic at the University of Massachusetts Medical School has done perhaps the most to promote mindfulness, which he defined in 1990 as 'the awareness that arises from paying attention in a particular way: on purpose, in the present moment, and nonjudgmentally'.

The benefits of mindfulness are clear in brain scans of new practitioners. After eight weeks, blood flow and tissue density improved in key neurological areas for focused attention. Even more amazing, mindfulness training can enact enduring change to your emotional set-point – your core degree of happiness. This discovery is

revelatory. Previously it was held that we are either innately cheery or melancholy, and that nothing could alter this fundamental emotional ecology. Although dramatically happy or catastrophic occurrences, such as winning the lottery or losing a loved one, would tilt our feelings, eventually we would revert to our prior emotional state. But mindfulness produces lasting emotional transformation, showing that we can boost enjoyment and resilience in small, practical steps.

Assuming that you can't take a two-year sabbatical in Walden Woods, you could live more deliberately while enjoying the comforts of the modern world. Thoreau's concept has been repackaged by Ryder Carroll, inventor of the Bullet Journal, who urges us to 'lead an intentional life', one in which our actions consciously align with our wishes.

There are many ways to incorporate this intentional approach into your day-to-day. Think on the lessons covered previously,

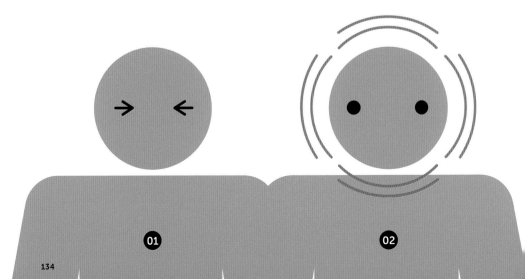

regarding pace and tempo; structuring and planning time; setting time pressures; living in sympathy with your body clock; quarantining distractions; protecting willpower; and cultivating space for spontaneity and fun. And keep examining your intentions: reflect on whether your daily choices accord with your goals.

To sharpen your consciousness-raising abilities:
> **Sign up to a mindfulness course**
> **Invest in a meditation app or Bullet Journal**
> **Try exercise classes such as yoga**

You can practice mindfulness any time, anywhere: on the bus, brushing your teeth, at work (although you might look like you've fallen asleep). According to Professor Katherine Weare of the University of Exeter and Southampton's mood disorder centre, the simplest tactic is to pause briefly in the middle of what you are doing and concentrate on your sensory perceptions. After two minutes your breathing will slow, your parasympathetic nervous system will kick into gear, and you will emerge refreshed and calm, ready to seize your next moment.

FOUR STEPS TO MINDFULNESS
01. **Close your eyes.**
02. **Attend to the sensation of your body – your feet on the floor, your bottom on the chair, the sounds that you hear.**
03. **Concentrate on your breathing: the rise and fall of your belly and chest, the air flowing through your nostrils.**
04. **Notice your thoughts. As they wander, acknowledge then redirect them to your breathing.**

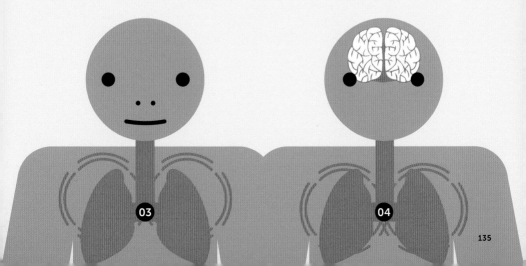

FUTURE PERFECT

Roam around any city in the developed world and you will discover pretty much every public space is mapped by time-management techniques, cunningly contrived to smooth the commercial flow. From traffic lights to tap-and-go payment devices designed to facilitate swift, unreflecting spending, to the escalators stationed at far-flung corners of the shopping centre aiming to herd you past as many retailers as can be, in the hope that while your distractible mind is wandering, something will catch your eye and lead your feet inside the store.

Yet we are not mindless consumers. Each of us has this remarkable talent for moving purposefully through time. Sometimes it can seem negative, particularly given that we are happiest when our mind is not wandering but 'in the moment'. However, the disruptive capability of our minds to roam beyond our immediate situation is boundless. We can picture something new, bigger or better, and bring it into being. We can travel vast distances, plan battles, build walls, plot coups. This is why our planet is scarcely recognizable from the one the first modern humans roamed 300,000 years ago.

Although we are all time machines, travelling through space, each of us has a different propeller. Some of us are present-focused, drifting with the current, others dragged by feelings rooted in the past, but most are driven by a combination of factors. Notice what influences you and you can dramatically change your circumstances, because as discussed in Lesson 11, your

temporal outlook skews your life prospects. Future-oriented individuals – those who save and plan, foregoing short-term pleasures for long-haul gains – tend to live longer, richer and healthier lives. Brain scans reveal that they also entertain warmer, friendlier feelings for their future selves than impulsive individuals, who struggle to extend this sort of imaginative hospitality, feeling little more sympathy for the wrinkly old person whom one day they will become than they would for a stranger.

So if you want to future-proof your life, practise moving your mind ahead. And note that mental time travel can make life better, whichever direction you take. For successful businessman David Alliance, the past provided more than a refuge. A trader in Tehran's Grand Bazaar from the age of fourteen, in 1950 Alliance turned eighteen and flew to Manchester with £14 in his pocket. There he built the largest textile company in the West. But as he grew older, time began to bite.

'When I was exhausted after a long day of doing business, I would close my eyes and become a little boy again in Kashan: the sun beat down on the courtyard of our family house. . . sometimes it brought sweat to my brow. My father and sisters were there, and there was love and laughter and security. When I opened my eyes, I would find myself back in an office in Manchester, but refreshed and full of energy, ready to get on with the task at hand. I did this even in board meetings and no one in the room ever guessed the journey I had just been on, or understood how I could recover my energies so rapidly.'

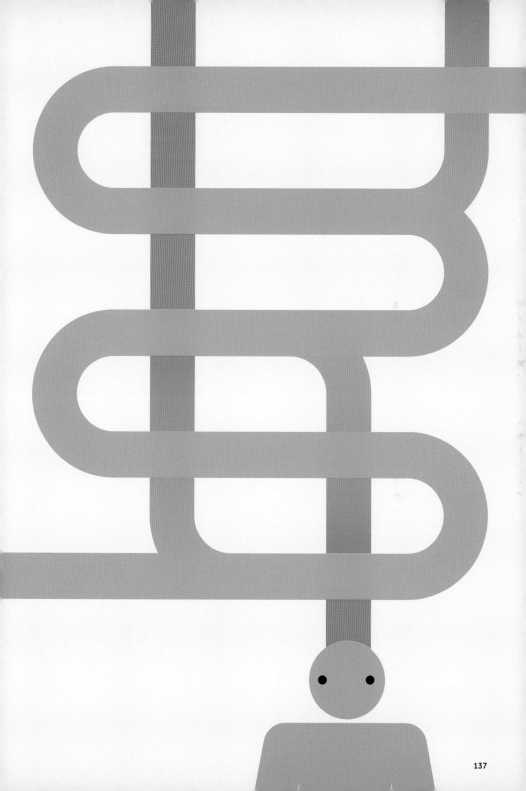

STRENGTHEN YOUR TIME MACHINE'S PROPELLER

You can improve your skills in mental time travel. Sports champions illustrate how visualization can be the midwife to success. For instance, training for the 1992 Olympics, 400-metre hurdler Sally Gunnell repeatedly pictured herself winning, mentally going through the perfect race, bound by gazelle-like bound, until finally she laced up her shoes to take gold. Similarly, when Team GB's youngest player, 25-year-old Hollie Webb, stepped forward for the deciding penalty in the 2016 Olympic women's hockey final, she knew that one strike could spell Britain's first victory or its greatest loss. She eyeballed the goalkeeper, swiped, and smack.

'I watched it go into the net and then I can't remember anything else since then,' she said afterwards. 'We practise them so many times and I just tried to imagine I was training at Bisham Abbey.'

By telling herself this was something ordinary, the latest in a line of similar moments, Webb robbed the moment of its pressure – allowing her to be extraordinary.

Make visualization a habit and it will add greater value. The clearer the picture, the firmer its contours, the more closely what you are hoping for will resemble something like destiny. If you make an art of this, far more than a tactic, it can become a strategy for life.

For instance, think about New Year's resolutions and bucket lists. Often these wish lists turn into guilt lists. But you can turn them into constructive plans for action. Like my inspiring friends, who on 1 January every year draw up a list, not of resolutions, so often a depressing parade of jilted pleasures, but of ambitions. They identify one aim for each of four areas: work, relationships, body and spirit. The rule is they can wish for anything at all, but it must be a reach beyond what is easily achievable. Then they write out a step-by-step plan to get there.

Every few months, they glance at the plans and compare notes. Come 31 December, champagne in hand, they exchange lists once more. Surprisingly often their goals have become a reality.

DREAM-LISTING

Why wait until 1 January? Start dream-listing now.

01. Identify four goals: for your career, relationships, health and soul.
02. What steps will get you there in a year?
03. Break down the steps into quarterly goals. Now break the quarterly goals into monthly goals. Finally, break monthly goals into week-by-week actions.
04. Decide when these weekly actions will happen.
05. Put them in your diary.
06. Each month, review your plans. Are you keeping up? Do you need to adapt? Should you speed up or slow down?

Remember there is nothing wrong with taking the scenic route to success. It might be more satisfying – and enduring.

We need all kinds of time – fast, slow, reflective, hedonistic – to live to the full. But life's greatest joy comes when we feel that we are directing our journey. What powers a wish is hope. So let that be your propeller. Can you see where you want to be? Now paint the picture, while the light lasts.

TOOLKIT

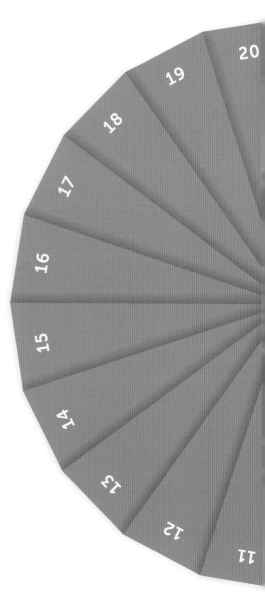

17

Pauses are easily overlooked, but crucial to our ability to focus. Taking a break also lends urgency to the time leading up to it, and can even offer an opportunity for your mind to catch up with a problem and come up with an answer. So analyze your day and truffle out those golden moments, the transitions and rituals that offer a change of gear. Can you increase their duration and frequency? Introduce a catnap and you will perform even better.

18

We look to pay and prizes to incentivize us, but intrinsic motivation – doing something for its own interest and pleasure – is far more powerful. Making work feel like a hobby may sound optimistic, but you can increase your sense of ownership. Decide how to tackle tasks, and design them so that you are always learning. Is it at a level that will stretch your skills? Are your goals clear? How do you measure success?

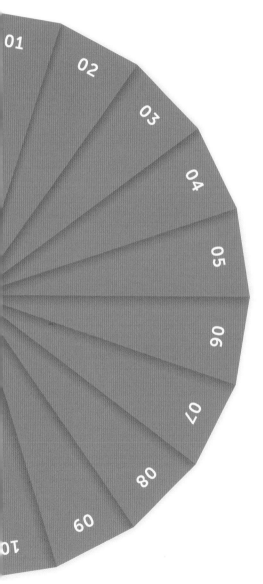

19

Today's world is present-drenched, as technology makes us prey to constant demands and distractions that fuel anxiety. Unfortunately, happiness is misunderstood. Studies reveal we are happiest when our mind is on what we are doing *in the moment when we are doing it*. But you can boost your happiness by practising mindfulness and by raising awareness of your daily choices to live more intentionally. Train your senses to be at peace in the moment. Pause, then breathe.

20

Future-oriented societies and individuals enjoy greater wealth and health. This serves as a reminder that although living in the moment is fun, it's self-defeating if you lose perspective on your long-term interests. Develop your skills of mental time-travel, using happy memories to boost your mood, and visualizing where you wish to end up — not just professionally, but spiritually, socially and physically. Draw up detailed plans, map the path, and you will get to where you want to go.

FURTHER LEARNING

READ

Start Where You Are
Pema Chödrön (Shambhala, 1994)

Finding Flow
Mihaly Csikszentmihalyi (Basic Books, 1997)

Daily Rituals
Mason Currey (Picador, 2013)

Rest: Why You Get More Done When You Work Less
Alex Pang (Basic Books, 2016)

Drive
Daniel Pink (Canongate, 2011)

WATCH

How To Lead An Intentional Life
Ryder Carroll
TEDxYale, YouTube

DO

Headspace app
Over three million users find this meditation aid alleviates stress, and even improves relationships.

Bullet Journal
An analogue solution to the problems of organising time in a digital world.

LISTEN

The Mindfulness Summit
www.themindfulnesssummit.com

Track Your Happiness App
www.trackyourhappiness.org

EPILOGUE

Next time you go online and contact dozens of friends, instantly, please pause to consider what a miracle this is.

Technology affords us extraordinary freedoms. We can custom-fit our day to suit ourselves. The danger of these superpowers is that inadvertently they render us deficient, as we race to keep up.

This book is your invitation to wonder: how can your freedoms with time liberate you?

It is worth reflecting on how far we have come since the Royal Mail relaunched in 1662, when a letter posted in London took up to 25 days to reach a city in Europe, the poor mail boy compelled to walk five miles an hour, even in darkest winter. As life sped up, time pressures increased, as novelist Thomas Hardy lamented, when Tess of the

D'Urbervilles ambles down a crooked street not 'made for hasty progress; a street laid out. . . when one-handed clocks sufficiently subdivided the day'.

Since those slow days, every technological leap forwards accelerated the rate at which actions can be performed. Sadly, this fluidity introduced new friction into our lives. 'Feeling rushed. . . causes people to buy more, pay more, try more things and more means to compensate for the stress, or at least to alleviate the anxiety,' wrote historian Margaret Visser. 'It also makes us work harder and longer – and therefore leave ourselves less time.'

Time pressure is horribly isolating. Yet I hope that I have convinced you that you are not alone. Universal biases and forces shape how you experience time. Understanding

'In truth, there is enormous space in which to live our everyday lives,' wrote Buddhist thinker Pema Chödrön. And she is right. We each possess twenty-four hours a day to work, rest and play. Nothing has changed since Epicurus, the first philosopher of pleasure, observed: 'Not what we have, but what we enjoy, constitutes our abundance.'

them uncovers tools for using it better. Once you recognize that to feel time-poor is quite different from having no time, then it becomes easier to notice how you throw away your precious hours. Do you undervalue other people's? Before you press send, ask yourself: is that message – the one that interrupts your friends – really necessary? What are you not doing as a result?

Time management techniques can get you some of the way out of the hurry trap. But managing time is also high maintenance. How much better to refine the rhythm of your life and let routines and rhythms do most of the organising for you?

So slow down. Raise your awareness of time. Now seize its riches.

BIBLIOGRAPHY

Ainslie, George, *Picoeconomics* (Cambridge: CUP, 1992)

Alexander, Bethan *et al,* 'Multi-Sensory Fashion Retail Experiences', *Handbook of Research on Global Fashion Management and Merchandising* (London: IGI Global, 2016)

Alliance, David and Ivan Fallon, *A Bazaar Life* (London: Robson Press, 2015)

Andreou, Chrisoula *et al,* eds., *The Thief of Time,* (Oxford: OUP, 2010)

Arstila, Valtteri and Dan Lloud, eds., *Subjective Time* (Cambridge: MIT Press, 2014)

Bar-Haim, Yair *et al,* 'When time slows down', *Cognition and Emotion,* 24 (2010)

Baumeister, Roy and John Tierney, *Willpower* (London: Penguin, 2012)

Beaman, C.P., Hanczakowski, M. and Jones, D.M., 'The effects of distraction on metacognition and metacognition on distraction: evidence from recognition memory', *Frontiers in Psychology* 5 (2014)

Beaumont, J. & Lofts, H, 'Measuring National Well-being – Health, 2013' *Office for National Statistics* http://www.ons.gov.uk/ons/dcp171766_310300.pdf

Boice, Robert, 'Quick Starters: New Faculty Who Succeed', *New Directions for Teaching and Learning* 48 (1991)

Boroditsky, Lera, 'Metaphoric Structuring: Understanding Time through Spatial Metaphors', *Cognition,* 75 (2000)

Bosker, Bianca, 'Facebook Now Takes Up About As Much of Our Time as Grooming or Chores', *Huffington Post,* 23 July 2014

Brooks, K. *et al,* 'Enhancing sports performance through the use of music', *Journal of Exercise Physiology,* 13 (2010)

Buckley, Ralf, 'Slow time perception can be learned', *Frontiers in Psychology,* 5 (2014)

Burgess, Helen J., 'Evening ambient light exposure can reduce circadian phase advances to morning light independent of sleep deprivation', *Journal of Sleep Research,* 22 (2013)

Burkeman, Oliver, 'Goals to Achieve? Will Telling Others Help?', *Guardian,* 27 June 2009

Burton, C.M. *et al,* 'The Health Benefits of Writing about Intensely Positive Experiences', *Journal of Research in Personality,* 38 (2004)

Carskadon, M.A. *et al,* 'Regulation of adolescent sleep: implications for behavior', *Annals of the New York Academy of Sciences,* 1021 (2004)

Chatfield, Tom, *How to Thrive in the Digital Age* (London: Macmillan, 2012)

Chui, Michael *et al, The Social Economy,* McKinsey Global Institute (July 2012)

Cialdini, Robert, *Influence* (London: HarperBusiness, 2007)

Colvile, Robert, *The Great Acceleration* (London: Bloomsbury, 2016)

Csikszentmihalyi, Mihaly, *Finding Flow* (New York: Basic Books, 1997)

Currey, Mason, *Daily Rituals* (London: Picador, 2013)

Danziger, Shai *et al,* 'Extraneous factors in judicial decisions', *PNAS,* 108 (2011)

Darley, J.M. *et al,* '"From Jerusalem to Jericho": A Study of Situational and Dispositional Variables in Helping Behaviour', *Journal of Personality and Social Psychology,* 27 (1973)

DeVoe, S.E. *et al,* 'Time is tight: how higher economic value of time increases feelings of time pressure', *Journal of Applied Psychology,* 96 (2011)

DeVoe, S.E. *et al,* 'Time, money, and happiness: how does putting a price on time affect our ability to smell the roses?', *Journal of Experimental Social Psychology,* 48 (2012)

Dill, Kathryn, 'You're Probably Checking Your Work Email On Vacation – But You Shouldn't Be, Study Shows', *forbes.com,* 17 June 2014

Dolan, Paul, *Happiness By Design* (London: Penguin, 2014)

Draaisma, D., *Why Life Speeds Up As You Get Older* (Cambridge: CUP, 2006)

Duhigg, Charles, *Smarter, Faster, Better* (London: William Heinemann, 2016);

Eastman, Charmane I. *et al.,* 'How to Travel the World Without Jet lag', *Sleep Medicine Clinics,* 4 (2009)

Eisenhardt, Kathleen M., 'Making fast strategic decisions in high-velocity environments', *Academy of Management Journal*, 32 (1989)

Emmons, R.A. *et al,* 'Counting Blessings Versus Burdens', *Journal of Personality and Social Psychology*, 84 (2003)

Epicurus, trans. Strodach, John K., *The Art of Happiness* (London: Penguin Classics, 2013)

Finn, Adharanand, 'Does music help you to run faster?', *Guardian*, 22 April 2012

Fleming, Amy, 'Screen Time v. Play Time', *Guardian*, 23 May 2015

Fonken, Laura K. *et al.,* 'Influence of light at night on murine anxiety- and depressive-like responses', *Behavioural Brain Research*, 205 (2009)

Forman, Helen, 'Events and children's sense of time: a perspective on the origins of everyday time-keeping', *Frontiers in Psychology*, 6 (2015);

Friedman, W.J. *et al,* 'Aging and the speed of time', *Acta Psychologica*, 134 (June 2010)

Glei, Jocelyn K., editor, *Manage Your Day-to-Day: Build Your Routine, Find Your Focus, and Sharpen Your Creative Mind* (Amazon Publishing: 2013)

Gleick, James, *Faster* (London: Abacus, 2000)

Griffiths, Jay, *Pip Pip: A Sideways Look at Time* (London: Flamingo, 2000)

Gross, Richard, *Being Human* (London: Routledge, 2012)

Hafner, Marco and Wendy M. Troxel, 'Americans don't sleep enough, and it's costing us $411 billion', *Washington Post*, 30 November 2016

Hallowell, Edward M., *Driven to Distraction at Work* (Brighton: Harvard Business Review Press, 2015)

Halpern, David, *Inside the Nudge Unit* (London: W.H. Allen, 2015)

Hammond, Claudia, *Time Warped* (Edinburgh: Canongate, 2013)

Hanh, Thich Nhat, *The Path of Emancipation* (Berkeley: Parallax, 2000)

Hart-Davis, Adam, *The Book of Time* (London: Mitchell Beazley, 2011)

Hern, Alex, 'Netflix's Biggest Competitor? Sleep', *Guardian*, 18 April 2017

Hochschild, Arlie, *The Time Bind* (New York: Metropolitan Books, 1997)

Hochschild, Arlie *et al*, *The Second Shift* (New York: Avon Books, 1990)

Humphrey, Nicholas, *Seeing Red* (Cambridge: Harvard University Press, 2008)

Jenkins, Allan, *Morning: How to Make Time. A Manifesto* (London: Fourth Estate, 2018)

John, Emma, 'GB women win historic hockey gold', *Guardian*, 19 August 2016

Jones, Luke A. *et al,* 'Click trains and the rate of information processing: Does "speeding up" subjective time make other psychological processes faster?', *Quarterly Journal of Experimental Psychology*, 64 (2011)

Kahneman, Daniel, *Thinking, Fast and Slow* (London: Penguin, 2012)

Kenney, Patrick J. *et al.,* 'The Psychology of Political Momentum', *Political Research Quarterly*, 47 (1994)

Killingsworth, Matthew A. *et al.,* 'A Wandering Mind Is an Unhappy Mind', *Science*, 330 (2010)

King, L.A., 'The Health Benefits of Writing about Life Goals', *Personality and Social Psychology Bulletin*, 27 (2001)

Kivimäki, Mika *et al.,* 'Long working hours and risk of coronary heart disease and stroke: a systematic review and meta-analysis of published and unpublished data for 603,838 individuals', *The Lancet*, 386, 31 October 2015

Klein, Stefan, *Time: A User's Guide* (London: Penguin, 2008)

Kruglanski, Arie W. *et al,* 'Experience of Time by People on the Go: A Theory of the Locomotion–Temporality Interface', *Personality and Social Psychology Review* (2015)

Layard, Richard, *Happiness* (London: Penguin, 2005)

Levine, Robert, *A Geography of Time* (London: Oneworld, 2006)

Levine, Robert V. and Ara Norenzayan, 'The Pace of Life in 31 Countries', *Journal of Cross-cultural Psychology*, 30, 2 (March 1999)

Mandela, Nelson, *Long Walk to Freedom* (London: Abacus, 1995)

Mark, Gloria *et al*, 'The Cost of Interrupted Work: More Speed and Stress', in *CHI '08 Proceedings of the SIGCHI Conference on Human Factors in Computing Systems* (New York: ACM, 2008)

Marquié, Jean-Claude *et al*, 'Chronic effects of shift work on cognition: findings from the VISA longitudinal study', *Occupational & Environmental Medicine*, 72 (2014)

Matlock, Teenie *et al.*, 'On the Experiential Link Between Spatial and Temporal Language', *Cognitive Science*, 29 (2005)

Milliman, Ronald E., 'The Influence of Background Music on the Behavior of Restaurant Patrons', *Journal of Consumer Research*, 13 (1986)

Mischel, Walter, *The Marshmallow Test* (London: Little Brown, 2014)

Moore, Don A. *et al.*, 'Time Pressure, Performance, and Productivity', in Volume 15, *Looking Back, Moving Forward: A Review of Group and Team-Based Research* (Bingley: Emerald Group Publishing Limited, 2012)

Mullainathan, Sendhil and Eldar Shafir, *Scarcity: Why having too little means so much* (London: Allen Lane, 2013)

Noone, Breffni M. *et al.*, 'The Effect of Perceived Control on Consumer Responses to Service Encounter Pace: A Revenue Management Perspective', *Cornell Hospitality Quarterly* (2012)

O'Brien, Edward H. *et al*, 'Time Crawls When You're Not Having Fun: Feeling Entitled Makes Dull Tasks Drag On', *Personality and Social Psychology* (2011)

Oeppen, J. *et al.*, 'Broken Limits to Life Expectancy', *Science*, 296 (2002)

Offer, Avner, *The Challenge of Affluence* (Oxford: OUP, 2006)

Panda, Satchidananda, http://www.salk.edu/news-release/more-than-3000-epigenetic-switches-control-daily-liver-cycles/

Partnoy, Frank, *Wait* (London: Profile, 2012)

Peterson, Dan, 'Music Benefits Exercise, Studies Show', *LiveScience.com*, 21 October 2009

Pink, Daniel, *Drive* (Edinburgh: Canongate, 2011)

Price, Michael, 'The risks of night work', *Monitor on Psychology*, 42 (2011)

Ramin, Cody *et al.*, 'Night shift work at specific age ranges and chronic disease risk factors' *Occupational & Environmental Medicine*, 72 (2014)

Randler, C. *et al*, 'Correlation between morningness, eveningness and final school leaving exams', *Biological Rhythm Research*, 37 (2006)

Roenneberg, Till, *Internal Time* (Cambridge: Harvard University Press, 2012)

Schöneck, Nadine M., 'Europeans' work and life – out of balance? An empirical test of assumptions from the "acceleration debate"', *Time & Society* (2015)

Seneca, *Moral Letters to Lucilius*, Letter 12

Sennett, Richard, *The Craftsman* (London: Penguin, 2009)

Spira, Jonathan B. *et al*, *The Cost of Not Paying Attention*, http://iorgforum.org/wp-content/uploads/2011/06/CostOfNotPayingAttention.BasexReport1.pdf; https://www.fastcoexist.com/1682538/stream-these-coffee-shop-sounds-to-boost-your-creativity; http://psych.cf.ac.uk/contactsandpeople/jonesdm.php

Steel, Piers, 'The Nature of Procrastination: A Meta-Analytic and Theoretical Review of Quintessential Self-Regulatory failure, *Psychological Bulletin*, 133, No.1 (2007) pp65-94

Sternberg, Robert J., 'The Theory of Successful Intelligence', *Interamerican Journal of Psychology*, 39 (2005)

Strogatz, Steven, *Sync* (London: Hachette, 2004)

Svendsen, Lars, *A Philosophy of Boredom* (London: Reaktion, 2005)

Syed, Matthew, *Black Box Thinking* (London: John Murray, 2016)

Talarico, Jennifer M. *et al*, 'Positive emotions enhance recall of peripheral details', *Cognition and Emotion*, 23 (2009)

Tate, Carson, *Work Simply* (London: Portfolio Penguin, 2015)

Tharp, Twyla, *The Creative Habit* (London: Simon & Schuster, 2007)

Thoreau, Henry David, *Walden* (London: Penguin, 2016)

Triplett, Norman, 'The Dynamogenic Factors in Pacemaking and Competition', *American Journal of Psychology,* 9 (1898)

Vanderkam, Laura, *What the Most Successful People Do Before Breakfast* (London: Portfolio Penguin, 2013)

Vida, Irena *et al,* 'The Effects of Background Music on Consumer Responses in a High-end Supermarket', *The International Review of Retail, Distribution and Consumer Research,* 17 (2007)

Wearden, J.H. *et al,* 'What speeds up the internal clock? Effects of clicks and flicker on duration judgements and reaction time', *Quarterly Journal of Experimental Psychology,* 70 (2017)

Weil, Zachary M. *et al,* 'Sleep Deprivation Attenuates Inflammatory Responses and Ischemic Cell Death', *Experimental Neurology,* 218 (2009)

Williams, Mark and Danny Penman, *Mindfulness* (London: Piatkus, 2011)

Williamson, Victoria, *You Are the Music* (London: Icon Books, 2014)

Wiseman, Richard, Pace of Life, http://www.richardwiseman.com/quirkology/pace_home.htm

Wiseman, Richard, *59 Seconds: Think a Little, Change a Lot* (London: Pan, 2009)

Wittman, Marc, 'Time Perception and Temporal Processing Levels of the Brain', *Journal of Biological and Medical Rhythm Research,* 16 (1999)

Wood, Linda, https://www.aspenideas.org/session/information-overload-can-we-still-be-productive-world-full-constant-updates

Yalch, R. *et al,* 'Effects of Store Music on Shopping Behaviour', *Journal of Consumer Marketing,* 4 (1990)

Zhong, Chen-Bo *et al.,* 'You Are How You Eat: Fast Food and Impatience', *Psychological Science,* 21 (2010)

Zimbardo, Philip and John Boyd, *The Time Paradox* (London: Rider, 2010)

At BUILD+BECOME we believe in building knowledge that helps you navigate your world.

Our books help you make sense of the changing world around you by taking you from concept to real-life application through 20 accessible lessons designed to make you think. Create your library of knowledge.

BUILD +
BECOME
www.buildbecome.com
buildbecome@quarto.com

@buildbecome
@QuartoExplores

Using a unique, visual approach, Gerald Lynch explains the most important tech developments of the modern world – examining their impact on society and how, ultimately, we can use technology to achieve our full potential.

From the driverless transport systems hitting our roads to the nanobots and artificial intelligence pushing human capabilities to their limits, in 20 dip-in lessons this book introduces the most exciting and important technological concepts of our age, helping you to better understand the world around you today, tomorrow and in the decades to come.

Gerald Lynch is a technology and science journalist, and is currently Senior Editor of technology website TechRadar. Previously Editor of websites Gizmodo UK and Tech Digest, he has also written for publications such as *Kotaku* and *Lifehacker,* and is a regular technology pundit for the BBC. Gerald was on the judging panel for the James Dyson Award. He lives with his wife in London.

GERALD LYNCH

BUILD +
BECOME

GET TECHNOLOGY

BE IN THE KNOW.
UPGRADE YOUR FUTURE.

KNOW TECHNOLOGY TODAY,
TO EQUIP YOURSELF FOR
TOMORROW.

Using a unique, visual approach to explore philosophical concepts, Adam Ferner shows how philosophy is one of our best tools for responding to the challenges of the modern world.

From philosophical 'people skills' to ethical and moral questions about our lifestyle choices, philosophy teaches us to ask the right questions, even if it doesn't necessarily hold all the answers. With 20 dip-in lessons from history's great philosophers alongside today's most pioneering thinkers, this book will guide you to think deeply and differently.

Adam Ferner has worked in academic philosophy both in France and the UK – but it's philosophy *outside* the academy that he enjoys the most. In addition to his scholarly research, he writes regularly for *The Philosophers' Magazine*, works at the Royal Institute of Philosophy and teaches in schools and youth centres in London.

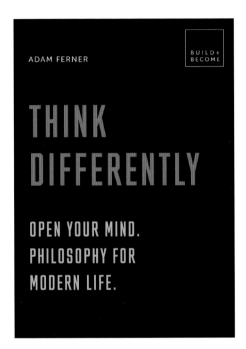

ADAM FERNER

BUILD + BECOME

THINK DIFFERENTLY

OPEN YOUR MIND. PHILOSOPHY FOR MODERN LIFE.

PHILOSOPHY IS ABOUT OUR LIVES AND HOW WE LIVE THEM.

Using a unique, visual approach to explore the science of behaviour, *Read People* shows how understanding why people act in certain ways will make you more adept at communicating, more persuasive and a better judge of the motivations of others.

The increasing speed of communication in the modern world makes it more important than ever to understand the subtle behaviours behind everyday interactions. In 20 dip-in lessons, Rita Carter translates the signs that reveal a person's true feelings and intentions and exposes how these signals drive relationships, crowds and even society's behaviour. Learn the influencing tools used by leaders and recognize the fundamental patterns of behaviour that shape how we act and how we communicate.

Rita Carter is an award-winning medical and science writer, lecturer and broadcaster who specializes in the human brain: what it does, how it does it, and why. She is the author of *Mind Mapping* and has hosted a series of science lectures for public audience. Rita lives in the UK.

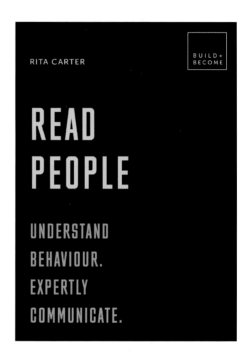

RITA CARTER

BUILD + BECOME

READ PEOPLE

UNDERSTAND BEHAVIOUR. EXPERTLY COMMUNICATE.

CAN YOU SPOT A LIE?

Using a unique, visual approach, Nathalie Spencer uncovers the science behind how we think about, use and manage money to guide you to a wiser and more enjoyable relationship with your finances.

From examining how cashless transactions affect our spending and decoding the principles of why a bargain draws you in, through to exposing what it really means to be an effective forecaster, *Good Money* reveals how you can be motivated to be better with money and provides you with essential tools to boost your financial wellbeing.

Nathalie Spencer is a behavioural scientist at Commonwealth Bank of Australia. She explores financial decision making and how insights from behavioural science can be used to boost financial wellbeing. Prior to CBA, Nathalie worked in London at ING where she wrote regularly for *eZonomics*, and at the RSA, where she co-authored *Wired for Imprudence: Behavioural Hurdles to Financial Capability*, among other titles.

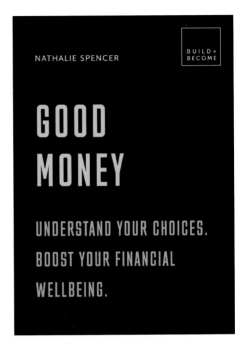

WE ALL MAKE CHOICES
WITH MONEY –
UNDERSTAND YOURS.

Through a series of 20 practical and effective exercises, all using a unique visual approach, Michael Atavar challenges you to open your mind, shift your perspective and ignite your creativity. Whatever your passion, craft or aims, this book will expertly guide you from bright idea, through the tricky stages of development, to making your concepts a reality.

We often treat creativity as if it was something separate from us – in fact it is, as this book demonstrates, incredibly simple: creativity is nothing other than the very core of 'you'.

Michael Atavar is an artist and author. He has written four books on creativity – *How to Be an Artist, 12 Rules of Creativity, Everyone Is Creative* and *How to Have Creative Ideas in 24 Steps – Better Magic.* He also designed (with Miles Hanson) a set of creative cards '*210CARDS'*.

He works 1-2-1, runs workshops and gives talks about the impact of creativity on individuals and organizations. www.creativepractice.com

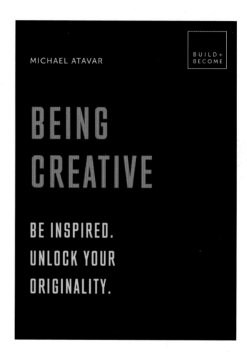

MICHAEL ATAVAR

BUILD + BECOME

BEING CREATIVE

BE INSPIRED. UNLOCK YOUR ORIGINALITY.

CREATIVITY BEGINS WITH YOU.

ACKNOWLEDGEMENTS

Thinking about time is a recipe for procrastination. Thank you to my wonderful editor Lucy Warburton, for her inspiration, patience and care, to the excellent Rachel Malig, for her laser-beam attention, and to Stuart Tolley, the designer responsible for making this book such an enjoyable looking read. Project editor Emma Harverson serenely brought all the pieces together under huge time pressure. The ideas in this book would not have been possible without the efforts of countless researchers and academics. Or without outsourcing some critical hours of domestic and family time to Wen Yi Lo, and to Sebastian Shakespeare. I am grateful for their understanding, and most of all, to Saskia and Rafael Shakespeare, whose delight in time multiplies mine a thousandfold.

Catherine Blyth is a writer, editor and broadcaster. Her books, including *The Art of Conversation* and *On Time*, have been published all over the world. She writes for publications including the *Daily Telegraph*, *Daily Mail* and *Observer* and presented *Why Does Happiness Write White?* for Radio 4. She lives in Oxford.